Police Personalities

Why Cops Act the Way They Do

STEPHEN M. HENNESSY, ED.D.

JAMES R. DELUNG, PH.D.

ISBN: Paperback   978-1-64184-736-0
        Ebook   978-1-64184-737-7

Laura Fry, PhD - Editor

Acknowledgements

I would like to express my sincere appreciation to the many law enforcement professionals, who, over the many years of my career, so willingly gave of their time to contribute to the contents of several books I have written on police personality involving an emphasis on the famous psychologist Carl Jung's theories on Personality Type. Of those, foremost would be the professionals at the Center for the Application of Psychological Type in Gainesville, Florida I worked with for many years in research with the MBTI®. They collaborated with me over twenty years ago on the third edition of "Thinking Cop Feeling Cop," the content of which is reflected in many parts of this book. I would like to specifically thank my many professional l colleagues including my co-author James DeLung, who I worked with at the Phoenix Police Department and Arizona Police Officers Standards and Training. He is a true professional and I am pleased he shared his vast expertise with me, making this book possible. I appreciated Thomas L. Reding, an executive with the St. Paul, Minnesota Police Department, for his intellect and insight; Hobart M. Henson, retired Assistant Director of the Federal Law Enforcement Academy, Glynco, Georgia, was the mentor who introduced me to the MBTI® and to other issues on developing leadership, which ultimately made several other publications possible. I also appreciate the interest and comments from many on our work, especially the support afforded us by William L. Tafoya, Ph.D., Professor Emeritus, University of New Haven, and an internationally recognized expert on the future of policing.

During my Law Enforcement career, I appreciated the countless opportunities that my colleagues at the Minnesota Bureau of Criminal Apprehension and the Phoenix, Arizona Police Department afforded me continue looking into the ramifications that cognitive styles have on our profession. I am especially appreciative of the support of Division Director Gerald Richard, II, Esq., as well as retired Training Bureau Commanders Donald Swanson and John L. Buchanan as I developed "The Law Enforcement Personality Profile® which measures Jungian cognitive Styles from a law enforcement point of view. The very capable leaders of these organizations included Chief Harold Hurtt, Chief Dennis Garrett, Superintendents Paul J. Tschida, Jack Erskine, and Mark Shields.

My subsequent teaching career at St. Cloud State University in Minnesota included mentorship and support from many, including Professors F. Barry Schreiber, John H. Campbell, Robert Prout and Stewart Wirth who are true professionals in their field of education.

Stephen M. Hennessy, Ed.D.

I am humbled by the incredible mentorship I have received during my professional career. As a young, high-speed, low-drag, police officer in the mid-1990's, my co-author Dr. Stephen Hennessy took interest in me. Dr. Hennessy asked if I would be interested in assisting with training a cultural awareness class throughout the Phoenix Police Department, and he taught me the curriculum from its inception through delivery to application. This was the beginning of my professional public speaking career. I cannot thank Dr. Hennessy enough for the confidence and passion he poured into my personal and professional lives.

My career-development mentors will always have a special place in my heart for teaching me service to others before self. Chief Steve

Campbell, Dr. Connie Kostelac, Lt. Stan Hoover, and Chief Rod Covey will forever have my gratitude.

My father, Richard DeLung, PhD was the greatest influence in my young life. He was the example for me to follow for my entire life. As a husband, father, professor, and head football/baseball coach as a child, my dad inspired me to be the man my family and friends would be proud to know. I will forever be thankful that my dad pushed me every day to be better than yesterday.

My wife Erin and son Ryan have been the greatest influence in the last decade of my life to reach further and represent the DeLung family name by mentoring others. With their incredible support, I was able to complete my Doctorate in Business Administration – Organizational Leadership and consulted all over North America. Thank you for being the best part of my life. I love you...

James R. DeLung, Ph.D.

Preface

Since the mid-1970s, two writing styles have predominated in discussions of police psychology, cognitive styles and personality assessment. The literature has tended to be either excessively academic or exceedingly mundane. This is, in part, why police administrators may make such little use of, or not even be familiar with Carl Jung's conceptual framework of cognitive styles measured by Law Enforcement Personality Profile® or other Jungian cognitive instruments such as the Myers Briggs Type Indicator™ available for study. Effectively explaining the complex nature of opposing characteristics in communication, perception and judgement from a Jungian viewpoint as well as the value systems of Millennials (those individuals born between the years of 1980-1995) that distinguish behavior of police is not easy. If the explanations are oversimplified, scholars quickly become bored, while practitioners believe they are being patronized and insufficiently informed to make applications of this important research.

It is little wonder then that authors have struggled with determining how best to present this important field of understanding police behavior through the eyes of personality or generational discussions involving those defined as "Millennials", those born between the years 1980 through 1995. The authors of this book have managed to avoid these pitfalls and to bridge the gap between theory and the "real world." Subsequently, this book neither insults the intelligence of scholars nor ignores the needs of practitioners.

The turbulent environment in which law enforcement currently operates draws close scrutiny and occasionally shrill criticism from the far right, the far left, and the political center. This makes it essential for field training officers, first-line supervisors, middle managers, administrators, and academy directors, as well as college and university faculty members, to develop a clear understanding of the various ways law enforcement officers assess problems that they confront on a daily basis. Of equal importance is learning to recognize the internal "drivers" that motivate individuals to do their very best. In short, leaders must be aware of their subordinates' cognitive preferences and personal value systems in order to draw more fully on their strengths.

This book, titled "Police Personalities; Why Cops Act the Way They Do", provides insights into why officers who usually perform brilliantly in many areas may perform poorly in certain other circumstances as well as what they really value as officers in paramilitary organizations. The book also sheds a great deal of light on the law enforcement profession and its interactions with the various diverse communities it serves. It is a very manageable book that presents rather complex material in a clear and concise manner. It is an exceptional presentation that would benefit any individual in the law enforcement profession.

William L. Tafoya, Ph.D.
Professor and Director of Graduate Programs in Criminal
Justice Emeritus
University of New Haven
West Haven Connecticut.
Founder - Society of Police Futurists International

Table of Contents

Part Three:
Understanding Police Through the
Millenial Generation in Policing

Appendices

Introduction

Law enforcement systems occupy an exceptionally unique position in our society. They represent a source of power that is not readily understood by many individuals. Agencies play a critical and necessary role in the preservation of public safety, maintaining public order, and enforcing the law. Police officers have often been the target of widespread complaint and criticism, particularly in recent years. Police officers have been characterized as being cold, condescending, matter of fact, and without compassion. They often seem to be at odds with the news media, social workers, and other helping professions. As our cities continue to become much more diverse, the conflict in communication with the various communities we serve is becoming an important issue.

As the majority of law enforcement executives realize, a law enforcement agency's most important asset is its employees. Agency leaders have a clear need to understand how their employees' function on the job, and how they work best while involved with the many tasks of policing.

Recruiting individuals for job functions related to policing is a continual challenge. Intelligence assessments, job interest, and physical agility tests, as well as personal interviews, are all used in various combinations. Recruiting efforts, however, may still target the wrong individuals for the job, or an individual may enter a profession and later realize that it was not the job they believed it to be. In addition to recruiting, the functions of training and motivating police officers are critical. Police agencies have a responsibility to understand the reasons for lack of motivation, low productivity, transfer and attrition rates, and poor performance among police personnel.

As all police executives know, being a law enforcement manager immersed in the daily happenings of the profession offers a unique insight into how people function in the occupation. To facilitate communication and to point out differences in Perception and Judgment in team-building exercises, the authors have been using the Law Enforcement Personality Profile® with attendees in various leadership classes and courses in developing cultural awareness and racial sensitivity. This inventory, based on Carl Jung's theories regarding personality type, helps people understand their preferred ways of taking in information and making decisions.

Knowing how individuals prefer to function in a Jungian Framework through the Profile can help police managers better understand the different ways their employees approach problems and the various strengths they use daily. This knowledge can be used to help understand why some police personnel function better in certain jobs than in others and why some officers may appear to be poorly suited for the occupation of policing. Insights can be gained into why police personnel look at crime and violators differently than many social workers, defense attorneys, representatives of the media, and psychologists. Additionally, it helps to gain insights on the police culture itself and interactions with diverse communities.

Because of teaching numerous leadership classes and watching the on-the-job behavior of those police executives attending, the importance of understanding the ways we function best in the profession has become evident. We have spent over twenty years conducting various studies on police personalities using the Law Enforcement Personality Profile®, as a basis for categorizing the differences we observed. Looking at the results continues to open a whole new dimension for better understanding the members of the law enforcement profession and their interactions among themselves and with the communities they serve. Even though the Law Enforcement

Personality Profile®, along with several other cognitive instruments were used in confirming various preferences in the way that people preferred to do things, it is not necessary for one to take the Profile to understand the contents of this book. Differences and similarities of behavior in individuals are very evident and easily understood by watching and listening to how other people communicate, the words they use and how they interact with their coworkers and perform their job functions. The important issue here is that there is a rational, understandable, reason people behave in certain ways. Knowing this can give us all an excellent tool to understand policing, police officers, and to perform our jobs better.

This book includes numerous observations that the authors have made in their many years in policing in federal, state and local law enforcement agencies. This includes experience as an officer on the streets in a major city police department, top level executive positions. years as the training advisor for a major city police department, years administrating training in a state level certifying board, years as a Special Agent with the FBI, and years in executive positions of a state level police agency. These observations reinforce our convictions that the understanding of Jungian Personality Styles in the law enforcement profession can only help to assist us as administrators in our leadership roles with our organizations and the communities we serve. The book includes communication styles, insights in motivation of those young officers described as "Millennials", and information on course methodology, and how to successfully present various course materials to law enforcement professionals.

The study of law enforcement and how we prefer to function can help executives in the profession to better understand their personnel and can give those individuals outside the profession insights into why police perform as they do. For the officer on the beat, understanding different ways their co-workers and others prefer to take in information and make decisions can help them deal with those differences better.

This book is written for police executives, the officer on the street, students of the law enforcement profession, representatives of the media, and other individuals involved in the various fields of law enforcement, public safety and civil and criminal justice. Because of the varied backgrounds of those who wish to expand their knowledge on police personality, the book has many facets. To the police administrators, the chapter on the police profession will be elementary and simplistic. It has been included to re-draft what the occupation is about from a lay person's point of view. The chapter on Jung's theory clarifies how he categorized the characteristics of individuals and the different ways they communicate.

We have included several appendices for those who may wish to read more detailed information on the Law Enforcement Personality Profile™, more complex police personality research, and ways to access materials for further training and development.

Stephen M. Hennessy, Ed.D.
James DeLung, Ph.D.

PART ONE

Understanding the History of American Policing

CHAPTER 1

Historical Perspective of American Policing

Contemporary American policing is structured from an evolution and mixture of styles from old English and Colonial America. Early American policing was carried out by volunteers from the community in order to police their own members. This style of policing was unorganized, without many rules and without purposeful policies. It appears early law enforcement was informal and communal, designed to meet the needs of each community with varying cultures, rather than utilizing wide-reaching policies, rules, and laws.

Colonial Policing

The disorganized policing of early America derived out of necessity in the port town of Boston, Massachusetts in 1631. Local ordinances were enforced by appointed constables who were just neighboring townspeople. These early lawmen were responsible for alarming the town of fires, maintaining health and sanitation, as well as capturing and bringing suspects to magistrates. This primitive style of law enforcement generally ran through the entire American Revolution. An innovative and organized law enforcement became necessary and was born out of the disorder of this historical time period.

The organized policing movement in America followed the British style known as the frankpledge system. In Britain, this semi-structured community policing was responsible for enforcing the local laws and dealing with stray animals. Men living in each of the communities would loosely organize in groups of ten called tithings with ten of these groups referred to as hundreds and then finally organized into shires. The shires of the time were similar to our modern-day counties in America. All law enforcement was in the responsibility of the shire reeve; hence the title sheriff was born in the United States. These new policing concepts shaped and evolved into constables, sheriffs, and community watchmen of Colonial America.

As new racial and ethnic group conflicts arose in Colonial America, slave patrols were created in the South. These patrols were specifically designed to maintain control over the slave population and evolved into policing indentured servants and then whites. Some literature identified these slave patrols as the first major organization of policing in America, while most other literature points to the early development of urban police departments. Either way, American policing continued to grow and evolve from contemporary issues.

Foundations of Modern Policing

Sir Robert Peel, the Home Secretary of England, is credited as the father of modern policing. He is the author of the Metropolitan Police Act to Parliament in 1829 which also led to the creation of the London Metropolitan Police that same year. The following nine Peelian Principles of Modern Policing are the foundation for all contemporary westernized law enforcement of today:

1. The basic mission for which the police exist is to prevent crime and disorder.
2. The ability of the police to perform their duties is dependent upon public approval of police actions.
3. Police must secure the willing co-operation of the public in voluntary observance of the law to be able to secure and maintain the respect of the public.

4. The degree of co-operation of the public that can be secured diminishes proportionately to the necessity of the use of physical force.

5. Police seek and preserve public favour not by catering to public opinion but by constantly demonstrating absolute impartial service to the law.

6. Police use physical force to the extent necessary to secure observance of the law or to restore order only when the exercise of persuasion, advice and warning is found to be insufficient.

7. Police, at all times, should maintain a relationship with the public that gives reality to the historic tradition that the police are the public and the public are the police; the police being only members of the public who are paid to give full-time attention to duties which are incumbent on every citizen in the interests of community welfare and existence.

8. Police should always direct their action strictly towards their functions and never appear to usurp the powers of the judiciary.

9. The test of police efficiency is the absence of crime and disorder, not the visible evidence of police action in dealing with it.

The nine Peelian Principles of Modern Policing directed early organizations, and they continue to be the cornerstone for law enforcement. Peel's principles are cross-cultural and relevant to all generations. The principles are timeless and universal, therefore just as applicable and necessary in today's historical and progressive police organizations.

Rapid urbanization of the early-established United States necessitated local and incorporated police organizations. The New York City Police Department was unified in 1845, followed by St. Louis in 1846, Chicago in 1854, and Los Angeles in 1869. These departments were developed more as a need to maintain order than they were as a response to criminal activity. During this rapid expansion of more modern police departments, the Peelian Principles were instrumental in the development of police responsibilities and new organizational policies. The early police departments all shared similar building blocks: (a) publicly funded, (b) bureaucratic in form, (c) full-time police employees, (d) department policies, and (e) accountable to the sponsored governmental authority. The publicly funded, bureaucratic police departments were established with community tax dollars and all organized in similar fashion. Full-time employees were accountable by rule of law under legal color of authority rather than untrained community volunteers. It is very likely that the Peelian Principles of modern policing were instructed to early police officers, and they continue to be taught in police academies nationwide as a historical perspective still valid today.

The direct involvement of politics in mid 1800s policing is evident in the historical literature. Politicians preferred police department to emphasize social control over labor workers rather than emphasis on controlling crime rates. The American Industrial Revolution brought about a class system of employers and employees that sometimes-found conflict with the local law enforcement. Therefore, business owners and politicians developed a reciprocal relationship with the police forces to keep the employees under control. Sometimes, entire police forces would change personnel with the new political leaders. Police departments of the time clearly worked for the business owners and politicians. Police departments would work under the authority from a local government and its politicians as an illusion of maintaining law and order. Public disorders such as drunkenness, political protests, and labor riots were classified as social disorder. Some literature explains the politician-controlled police of the time were actually the hench-men for early class warfare. The inferior of society were identified by their lack of skill, education, foreign status, ethnicity or skin color.

During the earlier days of modern policing, politicians became so powerful within police organizations; they directed their own police chiefs. These chiefs found they had very little influence over their own organizations due to the political stronghold of the politicians who appointed them. The tenure of a police chief was directly con-nected to the ability and willingness to play the political games of the time. The continued rise of police corruption at the organizational level was exacerbated by the direct connection to the politicians and wealthy business owners of the time.

Limited leadership and supervision of the police officers' daily duties led to further corruption and brutality in early American policing. No training or prerequisites existed for early police recruits. Hiring able-bodied males from the general community or relatives looking for work was standard practice. New police candidates and recruits who were willing to do the political bidding of the time were drawn in and hired. Workplace satisfaction and retention literature from early policing appears to be only about individuals willing to take orders from corrupt leaders and politicians were subsequently allowed to keep their jobs. When the only accountability for a police department's actions came from the elected politicians who controlled them, little to no trust was developed within the communities they served. Alcohol, bribery, gambling, prostitution, organized crime and intimidation of political party opposition became commonplace in many of the police department nationwide throughout the remainder of the 1800s. Unfortunately, policing had become embedded in the social behaviors of the time that they were entrusted to combat rather than strict adherence to the Peelian Principles of Modern Policing.

The early 1900s brought about police reform through the development of multiple commissions to investigate the efficacy of modern policing. The mission of the police reform commissions was to remove as much as possible the politicians and politics from American policing. Standards for hiring police recruits and administrators were now established rather than political appointees following a political agenda. The commissions were developed to clean up the current police organizations while creating professional police departments for the foreseeable future.

Additional important changes occurred within American policing in the early 1900s. Civil service systems were put in place for the hiring and promotions of police officers. This novel idea was designed to place the community internal to police departments and further remove the politicians. The civil service boards and rules also created hiring and training standards for police department through a series of best practices nationwide. Use of force training was also an instructional standard along with the other established police-specific training lacking from the past. Police communications also greatly improved. Call boxes and a two-way radio system began to emerge, which drastically improved efficiency and safety. Police administrators began to utilize a strategic police presence as a new model for proactively policing neighborhoods rather than the historically reactive style. These innovative changes in policing and police behavior were identified and necessary to combat the rampant corruption internal to organizations nationwide.

Police departments continued to face investigations designed to further professionalize and modernize them. The entire 1900s appeared to have commission after commission investigating, cleaning up, and prosecuting police individuals across the entire United States. Some major examples include: (a) Curren Committee in 1913 citing collusion with gambling and prostitution, (b) Seabury Committee in 1932 for prohibition corruption, (c) Knapp Commission in 1972 for gambling and drugs, and (d) Mollen Commission in 1993 investigated organized crime, excessive use of force, and drug use by police officers. These examples are provided in our book as evolutionary and historical accounts of improved police services that continue today. Historically, organizations have attempted to improve themselves from within the ranks as well. Police chiefs and leaders often appointed during or after scandals have made efforts and had successes in improving their police departments as well as the bureaucratic system itself. The continued improvements of police organizations from within were also directed at hiring practices, training standards, police policies, and the reduction of politics. Organization objectivity rather than political subjectivity became the new policing standard.

Professional Policing

The 1950s appears to be a significant historical time for American policing. The central theme for police departments of this time was crime control in a new paramilitary style. Police departments evolved into armed government officials in uniform with a rank structure that split their communities into beats for greater efficiency. Greater accountability and supervision arose from the new-found professionalism, and command and control of the police forces were centralized to a headquarters administration. Over a relatively short period of time, the aggressive paramilitary style and tactics of the 1950s police departments clashed with the members of their communities, especially minority citizens. When Rosa Parks was arrested in 1955 for failing to follow a segregation ordinance on a city bus, a community-organized boycott was instituted, and race relations with police greatly suffered. Whether protests were peaceful or not, some police agencies chose to arrest protest participants. During this historical time of policing, the professionalism of police departments was inward looking which isolated communities rather than include them until forced through federal and state legislation. Therefore, community-based policing was created as another evolution for the way law enforcement organizations should operate.

Community Policing

Community policing was developed as a result of lessons learned throughout the history of American policing. This policing method is not an altogether new style of policing, as some would label it, but it is a continual development of police operations as based on best practices nationwide. Sir Robert Peel's innovative principles of policing from 1829 are the cornerstone of contemporary community policing methods. Law enforcement officers during Peel's era were directed to be recognized in the public, obtain local information from the citizens, as well as recognize strangers from known faces in their assigned areas. Officers were supposed to be familiar with the neighborhoods and its normal activities to better identify deviant criminal behavior. This philosophy and proactive application of policing birthed the police beat system that is so familiar in American policing today.

When the Peelian Principles of Modern Policing are combined with police policies and practices, community policing ensues. "Community policing is, in essence, a collaboration between the police and the community that identifies and solves community problems" ("BJA Community Policing," 1994, p. vii). Community policing, community-based policing, and community-oriented policing are the most popular terms used to describe these modern police tactics, philosophies, and strategies. Whichever term is most appropriate or popular, they all illustrate police officers are no longer working to solve crimes and problems independently; the community is instrumental at all levels when community policing programs are active.

With an innovative emphasis of community members interacting with police officers, problems can be solved for current issues and create future community programs. An environment of trust between the community and its police officers is paramount for the success of community policing. Some communities may take longer to develop trusting partnerships for the full benefits of community policing. As stated previously, the historical perspective of policing amongst minorities and labor workers would explain how some communities or cultures are still suspicious of police organizations and their efforts to integrate community policing. Genuine working relationships between the police and the community could alleviate many community issues such as: (a) improved police community relations, (b) police decentralization, and (c) impact on how citizens feel about their communities rather than just focusing on crime rates. Historically, American policing reactively responded to all exigent issues in the community in conjunction with political bureaucratic changes rather than work with the community. Policing today is clearly more than dealing with criminal issues, but working hand in hand with the community for all issues.

Improved police community relations come from building trust through implementation and practice of the community policing model. More frequent interaction between police and the community will develop closer interpersonal relationships. Daily activities that place police officials and community members together to problem-solve develops greater trust. This trust, in turn, enhances daily communication as well as during times of crisis and chaos.

Police decentralization is a means of putting the problem-solving of community issues back into the hands of the community, such as Silent Witness. Silent Witness is a member of both Crime Stoppers USA and Crime Stoppers International. This program utilizes television and radio media outlets as a force multiplier for police agencies seeking help. The police department directly asks for the community's help in solving a recent or unsolved crime. Limited information about the crime is released to the community in effort to obtain greater leads for investigators to follow. Silent Witness offers communities members to assist in criminal investigations while maintaining their anonymity. This program also offers rewards to those who provide information that leads to arrests of suspects outstanding in criminal cases.

Community policing can greatly impact how citizens feel about living in their communities. Community policing is cooperative across a broad spectrum of issues affecting quality of life through community partnership and problem solving. As the social environment of America changes, so do the community policing philosophies. Single parent households have become more normal in society and children continue to be left alone more often. Immigrants, minorities, and ethnic groups are defining American life differently, and community policing efforts may qualitatively change community perceptions when appropriately launched and managed in the community.

Community policing is more than a philosophy. Practical application of programs supporting the philosophy is important to the success of community policing. Following the terrorist attacks of September 11, 2001, President George W. Bush created the USA Freedom Corps to develop greater volunteer programs nationally focusing on acts of service, sacrifice and generosity. The Citizens Corps provides volunteer opportunities to make communities safer and stronger with partnerships with local police agencies. This partnership became the Volunteers in Police Service (VIPS) which is managed by the International Association of Chiefs of Police (IACP). The Citizens Corps and the VIPS program build on successful efforts in nationwide communities to prevent crime and responder to disasters and emergencies. Police departments can contact the IACP for free information and policies for setting up VIPS programs in their communities. Online video training is also available for no charge to organizational leaders. Successful implementation of the VIPS programs requires relationship building and leadership.

Another popular and well-known community policing program is Neighborhood Watch by the National Crime Prevention Council. Released in 1972, Neighborhood Watch relies on citizens to organize themselves and work closely with local law enforcement to reduce crime and improve community awareness. The program is currently sponsored by the National Sheriffs' Association (NSA) which finds its roots back to Colonial America and the volunteer watchmen of the time who protected the community. The NSA uses the historical watchmen model with contemporary tools and technology through the community to improve community way of life.

Community policing does not mean police officers are no longer dedicated to fighting crime. Fighting crime should be incorporated into the goals and application of community policing with decentralized decision-making lowered to the street cop and community member. A combination of community input with police statistics and investigations may be the best combination for crime fighting and improving the way of life in the community. With the rapid police organizational and cultural changes, community policing has the ability to evolve with the people and the issues while continuing to solve problems and developing public trust. A genuine community policing effort is necessary from police leadership, officers, and the community for maximum effectiveness. A change in police tactics and philosophies usually goes hand in hand with a modification in police paradigms and culture.

Today's Technology and Policing

Social media is another example of police decentralization with community assistance. Millennial and Generation Z police officers are clearly comfortable with multiple versions of social media, and they have found a way to increase communication efficiency with the community. Crime tips, traffic jams, Amber and Silver Alerts have changed community policing through social media networks. Social media appears to be raising community policing to a new level by assisting direct communication between police departments and its citizens.

A BRIEF HISTORY OF

AMERICAN POLICING

Contemporary American policing is structured from an evolution and mixture of styles from Old English to Colonial America.

1631

Boston, MA: Local ordinances enforced by appointed constables (neighboring townspeople). Responsible for:
- alarming town of fires,
- maintaining health & sanitation,
- capturing/bringing suspects to magistrate

AMERICAN REVOLUTION

Organized Policing movement followed British style of frank pledge system (semi-structured community policing: enforce local laws & deal with stray animals)

Slave patrols, designed to maintain control over slaves, evolved into policing **Indentured Servants and white populations**

COLONIAL AMERICA

New policing concepts: constables, sheriffs, and community watchmen

1829

Father of **Modern Policing**, Sir Robert Peel, authors Metropolitan Police Act to England Parliament - led to creation of London Metropolitan Police the same year

1845

NYC Police Department unified **Need to maintain order** (not response to criminal activity)
St. Louis: 1846
Chicago: 1854
Los Angeles: 1869

MID 1800

Politics involved with policing
Emphasize social control over labor workers (rather than controlling crime rates)

EARLY 1900

Police Reform
Commissions to remove politics and politicians from policing **Civil service systems** established for hiring & promotion of officers

1950

Paramilitary style crime control: rank structure, communities split into beats, command & control of police forces centralized into headquarters administration

Community Policing

Modern Police philosophies, tactics, and strategies. Police decentralization = problem-solving community issues back into community hands (e.g., Silent Witness, Crime Stopper)

CHAPTER 2

Westernized Law Enforcement Profession and Culture

People tend to view police more as crime fighters rather than guardians of the public's safety, because this is an era of violent crime. The headlines of any newspaper are full of stories of violence that occurred the night before in any city, not only in this country, but throughout the world. Because we live with instant communication, news of schoolyard shootings, criminal bombings and other acts of criminal violence and terrorism are broadcast throughout the United States immediately. For various reasons, including the continuing epidemics of Opioid abuse, crack cocaine, methamphetamine, and other mind-altering substances, crime in the United States has become increasingly more violent in many ways.

The real job of policing is far different from some media portrayals in the newspapers, radio or on television. As stated by James Q. Wilson, a pragmatic, highly respected professor of government at Harvard, most police calls for assistance have little to do with crime and a lot to do with medical emergencies, family quarrels, neighborhood disputes, auto accidents, barking dogs, minor traffic violations, and similar events. Those calls that do involve actual felony crimes, such as burglaries, robberies, and auto thefts, typically occur long after the event has taken place.

As a democratic republic, we are heavily dependent upon police to maintain the degree of order necessary to make a free society possible. Herman Goldstein, scholar and police researcher, commented that police prevent people from preying on each other, provide a sense of security, facilitate movement, resolve conflicts, and protect the rights of free elections, free speech, and freedom of assembly on which the continuation of our free society depends. The strength of a democracy and the quality of life enjoyed by its citizens are determined in large measure by the ability of the police to discharge their duties. The average citizen thinks of police work as primarily concerned with preventing crime and apprehending criminals. When crime increases, or a particularly heinous crime is committed, the public usually calls for more or better police personnel. Conversely, when crime declines in a certain area, the police often get, or may try to take, the credit.

Law enforcement officers represent a fascinating anomaly in the United States. They are vested with an enormous amount of power and authority in a government founded under a system that generally dislikes and fears centralized power. The specific authority they possess to use force, detain, arrest, and search people can be awesome.

The relatively new concept of "The Ferguson Effect", coined by noted Criminal Justice Researcher Heather MacDonald, has contributed significantly to the challenges police face in trying to maintain order. The flood of such news greatly heightens our awareness and concern about crime. We watch numerous television shows that show cops moving in nonstop action for sixty minutes at a time (with appropriate breaks for commercials). On television a police radio report is received over the air and the officers speed through the streets (red lights on and sirens screaming), come to a tire-screeching halt, bail out of the cruiser (usually while it is spinning on its top after a spectacular crash), chase a violator down an alley into a dead end and either square off into a fight or pull him or her down from a chain link fence.

The scenario poses an exciting and interesting plot line, but may be more than inaccurate in the clear majority of cases. As for the recent phenomenon of video-taped true life action police and rescue shows, such as Cops and True Stories of the Highway Patrol, police are viewed as rolling from call to call in non-stop action on a daily basis. Much more action occurs in the larger cities than in the smaller jurisdictions, but most law enforcement officers from all departments get plenty of action. Somewhat differing from the media's non-stop action-filled portrayal of police work, Charles Saunders, another police researcher, compiled a lengthy list of attributes and skills years ago that a police officer must have to perform the job of policing. These include the ability to:

- Endure long periods of monotony during routine patrol, yet react quickly and effectively to a problem situation on the street or to the radio dispatcher;

- Gain extensive knowledge of the patrol area, not only the physical characteristics, but the normal routine of events, and the usual behavior patterns of its residents;

- Exhibit initiative, problem solving capacity, effective judgment, and imagination in coping with numerous and varying situations involved in a daily shift: a family disturbance, a potential suicide, a robbery in progress, a traffic accident, a medical emergency, or a disaster (police officers refer to this as having a lot of "common" or "street" sense);

- Make prompt and effective decisions, sometimes having to do with life or death, and be able to evaluate a situation quickly and take appropriate action;

- Demonstrate mature judgment as to whether an arrest is warranted or not, whether to warn or let go, or be willing to take control and use any physical force necessary to control the situation;

- Demonstrate critical awareness in discerning signs of conditions that are not ordinary, or circumstances that may indicate a crime is in progress;

- Exhibit several complex psychomotor skills such as driving a vehicle in emergency situations, firing a weapon accurately under extreme and varied conditions, and maintaining agility, endurance and strength in taking an individual into custody while using the minimum force necessary;

- Exhibit a professional, self-assured presence and a self-confident manner in dealing with offenders, the public, and the courts;

- Be capable of mediating a family dispute, handling neighborhood problems, and dealing with street gangs;

- Maintain objectivity when working with a host of special interest groups such as the press, family, victims, and offenders; and

- Maintain a balanced perspective in the face of exposure to the worst side of human nature.

These set of skills require a tactical understanding of policing and an empathic understanding of human relationships. Police communication preferences sometimes may appear to be different from how the community may prefer to communicate.

Law Enforcement Culture

Police culture is unique to those who work in a law enforcement capacity. Culture is loosely defined as the acceptable way of thoughts, beliefs, and behavior of a particular group which is passed on to succeeding generations. Often law enforcement culture is characterized by the public, police administration, and other police officers as hostile, untrustworthy and the system "is out to get them." The characterization of police culture is inherently influenced by the three forms of police culture: Organizational attributes are perpetuated by (a) artifacts, (b) embedded values, and (c) fundamental assumptions.

Artifacts

Police artifacts are highly recognizable and support pride and honor across the law enforcement industry. Artifacts are tangible items that promote the police structure such as the badge, gun, marked patrol cars, and methods of coded speech. These items appear to be utilitarian and passed on through generations of peace officers. For example, the culture of a police officer's uniform is different than a costume, because the uniform represents an entire industry and is role-filling rather than role-playing.

Historical artifacts for policing have both positive and negative effects on specific police agencies and the entire law enforcement industry. From the Colonial American slave patrols to the police conflicts of the American civil rights movement, analysis of police tools by many minority cultures has been negative. For example, a police baton carried for hundreds of years by police officers worldwide can be viewed as a negative artifact by community members due to historical events such as slave control, union busting, and the highly publicized Los Angeles Police Department Rodney King incident in 1993. Whether positive or negative, these tangible artifacts of policing should support the optimistic and constructive embedded values of the industry.

Embedded Values

Embedded values, such as integrity and justice, guide the subculture of law enforcement. New officers learn rules and procedures from the policy manual, but they learn the ways of policing from trainers and fellow officers. For example, a statutory government agency that develops and maintains the embedded values of sworn peace officers is the Arizona Peace Officer Standards and Training Board (AZPOST). The mission of the Arizona Peace Officer Standards and Training Board is to foster public trust and confidence by establishing and maintaining standards of integrity, competence, and professionalism for Arizona peace officers and correctional officers, and its vision is to produce and maintain the most professional peace officers in America. AZPOST was originally developed to attend to the need for minimum peace officer selection, recruitment, retention and training standards. AZPOST also provides curriculum and standards for all certified law enforcement training facilities statewide. The embedded values within the police culture of Arizona begins with AZPOST. When properly nurtured by police organizations, embedded values then become fundamental assumptions for all police officers. All states have various certifying or licensing agencies for law enforcement and public safety agencies.

Fundamental Assumptions

Fundamental assumptions of policing, such as courage, autonomy, and confidentiality, are the ethos of policing. The spirit of policing is service and sacrifice. This sacrifice is often manifested through the officer's health or life. Police work environments are filled with daily stressors both internal and external to the organization. It is reasonable to assume the command-and-control structure of policing negatively affects the overall morale and satisfaction of police organizations. Officers often historically reflect internal departmental issues as the greatest area of dissatisfaction in their careers. When confidentiality is turned into secrecy to protect one's self or partner, this becomes a negative infestation in policing and violates the fundamental core of police culture.

Organizational trust is a fundamental element of any police agency because of the many organizational benefits, such as employee commitment, satisfaction, and performance. Police organizations are unique in daily operations when compared to civilian occupations due to the very nature of how trust is understood and engaged. Historically, police organizations' handle decision-making, discretion, and control through centralized and Para militaristic means.

Policing is mainly a paramilitary-bureaucratic culture rather than collaboration. In the military, members are trained to deal with the intense stressors of the job knowing it most likely will be for a few years. Unlike the military, police departments train their personnel for the unique job stressors for what could be over 20 years. Many cops would say they are just learning the job after a few years, so how does a member of policing go from rookie status loving the job to veteran status hating the job and excited to retire?

Military and police-type organizations develop and maintain trust as a vital part of their culture. Increased mutual interdependence is mandated in police culture due to increased personal risk and vulnerability to daily tasks. Sworn officers' exposure to high risks daily greatly impacts interpersonal relationships and trust. Research indicates sworn police officers spend more time with other police officers outside of the work environment when compared to their civilian counterparts. These extended hours created stronger social relationships, therefore greater trust. The social cohesion developed in police organizations is vital to maintain positive culture.

The hierarchical police structure is designed to instill discipline throughout its ranks. Discipline to follow orders and tow the company line can cause internal organizational strife. In an occupation such as policing, severe extremes exist in the daily work from boredom to sheer terror. Policies and procedures combined with police embedded values do not always properly address the negativity. More progressive departments could find success by identifying preferred communication styles and adopting mentoring actions to repair trust rather than direct behavioral change through discipline.

The idea of procedural justice refers to one's perception of fairness and decision-making within an organization. Research of paramilitary organizations has identified a level of dependence from employees to employer for daily activities, pensions, and healthcare benefits that fosters a strong identity and loyalty. When police officers lose faith in their leaders or the system they depend upon, satisfaction and loyalty are diminished. Trusting relationships between police officers and their supervisors is paramount for a positive organizational culture. The high level of stress in police work makes this relationship especially important. The positive and negative perception of police supervisors is impactful on employees. Perceived negative feelings toward a supervisor become a burden, while the presence of an engaged and personable leader positively affects organizational commitment and morale of police officers. A police organization void of trust amongst its members could result in a very negative culture and low employee satisfaction and morale.

As noted earlier, the historical shift to police professionalism had unintended organizational culture consequences. Agencies became divided into old-timers and more progressive college-educated officers. The us versus them mentality historically socialized officers to rely on a cops versus criminals culture, yet a new divisive culture has shifted inside police organizations based on seniority, education, sworn status, and rank. Internal organizational strife has become the norm in American policing, and properly communicating is paramount. Organizational stress and line-employee opposition has a historical stronghold on police culture. In a survey of 2,500 police officers, noted author Neal Trautman found the majority of the 10 greatest sources of anger and low satisfaction came from police administrators, not daily police duties or citizens. Therefore, a culture of low job satisfaction appears to be greatly affected by police decision-makers through poor communication, inconsistent employee discipline and supervisory politics within the organization.

Many police culture typologies exist that separate officers from each other and the community. These typologies explain how officers are able to exist and survive in distinctly different worlds. For example, an intuitive thinking street cop may conflict with a feeling community relations officer which may then create an internal opposition of "us versus them." An us-versus-them and we-they worldview is pervasive in policing and anthropologically passed on through generations of cops internal and external to the organization. Generationally speaking, communicating the typologies across all of the generations appears to be an issue due to distinctly different worldviews. The cultural phenomenon of us versus them (internally and externally) will be addressed in our Law Enforcement Personality Profile®. This instrument explains what appears to divide officers from each other inside the department as well as from the community in which they serve.

Combining Tactical Necessity and Community Relations Approaches

The characteristics of law enforcement, described previously, are basic to the job of policing, regardless of the nature and size of the community policed. The reality of policing, however, offers an interesting and growing paradox, that of the need to be tactically aware and prepared for any violent event involving homeland security. Such events may call for tactical units like S.W.A.T. and bomb squads. Disturbances in major cities, involving real or perceived police excessive use of force, may negatively influence perceptions within the community. As such, attention to the needs of the community may occur through programs such as School Resource Programs, Gang Resistance and Education Programs, D.A.R.E., Community Awareness and Neighborhood Policing, and Bike Patrols.

William L. Tafoya, Ph.D., the founder of the Police Futurists Society International and a highly respected expert on the future of policing, predicted in his landmark Delphi study of the future of policing that this country may face possible riots and disturbances in coming years that will make the riots of the 1960s pale in comparison. The reasons for these problems are many but include the changing demographics of our cities and other socio-economic pressures and the constant harping of the media and politicians on income inequality. Tafoya's prediction, obviously, calls for being tactically prepared to meet these challenges. The paradox involves the pull of resources and job descriptions from opposite ends of the spectrum: being tactically prepared and interacting with the citizens. The tactical programs are attractive and involve high drama to both citizens and employees within law enforcement departments. However, Tafoya states those departments paying attention to the seemingly mundane daily tasks of working and interacting with many diverse community programs are those that are not going to have the serious riots and problems. Departments that focus on an "Us-Versus-Them" battlefield mentality will likely experience community disruption.

There are job tasks that are critically important to the job of policing that involve duties other than enforcing the law. Those involve the administrative functions of the department itself, as well as police and community relations and interacting with the community. As police administrators know, areas such as personnel, employee assistance, labor relations, planning and research, training, organizational development, and recruiting are also critical to the operations of any law enforcement organization. In many instances, the skills called upon to perform these functions may differ greatly from those called upon for the performance of the typical street policing function.

Many police know officers who perform satisfactorily on the street, but don't "set the world on fire." These same officers receive an assignment in other areas of the department and start performing like star quarterbacks. Because the individuals in question had an opportunity to use their natural strengths, they performed well. If the tasks of both assignments were analyzed, we would find that they were vastly different. Being able to chart some of our strengths and possible weaknesses by understanding different personality types and generational cohorts will contribute to understanding why people don't seem to do well at some tasks and yet excel at others.

PART TWO

Understanding Police Through Carl Jung's Theories of Personality Type

CHAPTER 3

Understanding Carl Jung's Theory

Carl G. Jung, a Swiss physician and psychologist, was a contemporary and associate of Alfred Adler and Sigmund Freud. During the late eighteen hundreds, Freud and Adler were eminent psychologists and researchers of their day. Jung observed great disagreements between them in their understanding of how people used their thought processes. Although the actual substance of the disagreements between the two psychologists were unimportant, Jung found them to reflect attractively simple differences in the way each looked at things. While individual personalities were complex, Jung considered the patterns among personalities an interesting phenomenon.

Concerning personality, the general scientific thought of the time was the environment influenced personality more than inheritance. Contrary to the thinking of the day, Jung felt that a person's psychological type was a product of genetic patterns and, at birth or shortly thereafter, the determinant of the way a person preferred to function in the world. As evidence, two people, from the same basic background and environment, could approach an issue from two completely different points of view.

To this day, scientists and psychologists still debate the issue of "nature" (inherited characteristics) or "nurture" (forces of the present environment); which has more to do with the development of personality? Many assume a combination of both factors shape the personality of an individual. Yet, consider the scenario of two children of the same sex born nine months apart to the same parents in the same environment and socio-economic factors. When asked to comment about the children's personalities, the mother or father likely state the children are completely different from each other, and they noticed the difference within days after the birth of the second child! Jung's theory of psychological types is a useful way of understanding the difference; genes are much more likely to affect personality development than environment.

The Four Functions: Mental Processing

In 1921, Jung's book *Psychological Types* was published explaining his theory. Jung identified four basic functions that structured an individual's personality; two functions were involved in the incorporation of information, labeled Perception, and two functions involved decision making, labeled Judgment. He believed people took in information in two ways, through Sensing or through Intuition, which he called Perceiving functions. According to Jung, people naturally had a preference for assimilating information and, after accessing this information, a decision was made. Reaching the conclusion was accomplished through one of two processes, Thinking or Feeling, which were called Judging functions. The four possible combinations of Perception and Judgment were Sensing with Thinking (ST), Sensing with Feeling (SF), Intuition with Thinking (NT), and Intuition with Feeling (NF). Jung felt these functions were an integral part of a person's personality and resulted in certain patterns of behavior which could be classified.

The Perceptive Functions of Taking in Information: Sensing or Intuition

In Jung's system, individuals experience the world through their Perceptive function, which is the taking in of information either by Sensing or Intuition.

Sensing types (S) use both Sensing and Intuition, but prefer and develop the use of Sensing which becomes the stronger and preferred function. Sensing types gain information through sight, sound, taste, smell, and touch. People preferring Sensing generally see only what exists at the immediate time. Strengths usually associated with this function are practicality, being very realistic, and being grounded in the present with a great aptitude for detail. In careers, higher Sensing scores correlate with engineers, bankers, accountants, those in various hands-on trades, and those professions requiring a close attention to detail.

Intuitive types (N) use both Sensing and Intuition, but prefer Intuition, which is seeing things in a more generalized, global way. The person who is using this function is less aware of specific details, but sees abstract patterns and relationships. Strengths usually associated with Intuition are creativity, global thinking, planning and research skills, and being able to see patterns and relationships. In careers, higher Intuition scores correlate with psychologists, artists, reporters, university educators, and those professions calling for abstractions and patterns or symbols.

The preference for the use of one over the other can be visualized as being on a continuum, with Sensing at one end and Intuition on the other. When we are taking in information, we are using the processes of Sensing or Intuition. We are using one or the other at a time, though, not both simultaneously.

Sensing   Intuitive

Jung felt that the preference for one over the other was "constitutional" or occurring at or near birth. One way to understand the preference issue better is for you to take a pen or pencil in your dominant hand, usually the right, and then sign your name. Then, transfer the pen or pencil to your other hand, usually the left, and write it again. You may groan and complain or laugh at the effort it takes and you may say you can't do it. Of course, you can, even though it usually does not appear as well written as when your dominant hand was used. This exercise illustrates how inborn preferences become stronger with use and those less used are not as well developed. Jung stated that people prefer a specific way of perceiving, either through Sensing or Intuition. He said that when we use that preference repeatedly, we become more familiar with that preference and more confident with its use. Most of us fall within the continuum, with one preference stronger than the other.

Typically, if people prefer the Intuitive function over the Sensing one, they concentrate on the total picture, but may tend to miss detail. On the other hand, if people perceive in specific detail, they tend to overlook the total picture.

The Judgment Functions of Deciding: Thinking or Feeling

Jung believed that the information acquired through Perception undergoes a "distillation" process through which an individual can make various decisions. As with taking in of information (Perception), Jung believed that people make decisions (Judgment) through one of two preferred functions, Thinking or Feeling.

Deciding through Thinking means you decide about a matter in a very analytical and impersonal way without necessarily taking into consideration the impact on the people involved. Thinking types (T) use both Thinking and Feeling but prefer Thinking for making judgments. Strengths developed from the use of Thinking as a judgment preference include objectivity, impartiality, a sense of fairness and justice, and skill in applying logical analysis. In careers, higher Thinking scores correlate with engineering, math, business, technical fields, sciences, and hands-on trades.

Feeling types (F), on the other hand, use both Thinking and Feeling, but prefer to reach judgments through Feeling. They tend to employ a process of reasoning which involves taking people into consideration first. Strengths typically associated with the use of Feeling as a judgment preference include an understanding of people, a desire for harmony, and a capacity for warmth, empathy, and compassion. In careers, higher Feeling scores correlate with professions dealing with social service, religious activities, teaching, and health care.

Thinking   Feeling

The Dominant and Auxiliary Processes

To understand how the functions work with each other during our daily lives, we need to understand the way the Perceptive and Judgment functions work together. One function will be dominant, the other one the auxiliary process.

If the dominant process is a Judging one (Thinking or Feeling), the auxiliary process must be a Perceiving one (Sensing or Intuition). Likewise, if the dominant process is a Perceiving process, obviously the auxiliary needs to be a Judging one. As an example, if a person's dominant function is a Perceiving one of Intuition, the auxiliary function must be a Judging function (either Thinking or Feeling). Logically it cannot be another Perceiving function as the information has already been perceived through Intuition. Besides serving as a complement to the dominant process, the auxiliary serves as a balance between Extraversion and Introversion.

Some individuals may dislike the idea of one process being more dominant than the other and prefer to think of themselves as using all functions equally well. Jung thought, however, that such impartiality kept all the functions relatively undeveloped and produced a "primitive mentality," because opposite ways of doing the same thing will interfere with each other if none has a priority.

Extraversion and Introversion

Jung further theorized the existence of Introversion and Extraversion, which he called "attitudes." Extraverts typically focus on the outer world, while Introverts are more comfortable focusing on their inner world of thoughts and ideas. Because the focus of this book is to look at the various ways officers differed in the ways they preferred to take in information and make decisions, we did not specifically mention the way Extraversion and Introversion play out in communication. However, during interviews with officers, we kept Extraversion and Introversion in mind. For example, if people preferred Introversion, we would just wait as they internally formulated their answers. If they preferred Extraversion, we would banter back and forth with them until they arrived at a conclusion about an issue we were discussing.

The Basis for Understanding This Section of the Book

As stated earlier, two possible preferences a person could use in taking in and processing information (Perception) were through one's five senses (Sensing) or through abstract patterns and relationships (Intuition). Two possible ways that a person could prefer to make decisions (Judgment) about a matter would be through either impersonal logic (Thinking) or personal evaluation of impact on people (Feeling).

The four combinations of those processes, which can be referred to as cognitive styles, are defined as follows:

Perception	Judgment	Style	Behaviors
Sensing	Thinking	ST	Practical, Matter of fact
Sensing	Feeling	SF	Sympathetic, Friendly
Intuitive	Feeling	NF*	Enthusiastic, Insightful
Intuitive	Thinking	NT*	Logical, Ingenious

*The letter "N" is used to denote Intuition, to keep from confusing Intuition from Introversion. Introversion is mentioned in this chapter, but the concept is not used as a basis for understanding the Cognitive Personalities referred to in this book. Jung believed Extraversion and Introversion were important in human functioning, but not deemed necessary in the construction of this book.

Each cognitive style is characterized by a variety of behaviors that a person demonstrates over a period of time. Others in the field called the ST combination practical and matter-of-fact, the NT combination logical and ingenious, the SF combination sympathetic and friendly, and the NF combination enthusiastic and insightful. Each one of us is an individual. However, since we share preferred ways of doing things with many others, we share certain common characteristics. These characteristics can be quantified and can help us do a much better job in relating to and understanding one another.

CARL JUNG

Mental Processing Preferences

Perceptive Functions of Taking in Information (Sensing or Intuitive)
Judgment Functions of Deciding (Thinking or Feeling)

S ### Sensing

Gain Info: Via senses (sight, touch, sound)
Sense of Time: Here & Now, Immediate
Strengths: Realistic, Details, Practicalities
Career examples: Banker, Accountant

N ### Intuition

Gain Info: Abstract, Patterns, Relationships
Sense of Time: Generalized, Global
Strengths: Research skills, Planning
Career examples: Artists, Psychologists

T ### Thinking

Decision making: Analytical, Impersonal
Strengths: Objectivity, Impartiality, Sense of fairness and justice, Apply logical analysis
Career examples: Engineering, Business

F ### Feeling

Decision making: Consider people first
Strengths: Understand people, Desire for harmony, Capacity for compassion, Warmth
Career examples: Healthcare, Teaching

A ### ATTiTUDES

Introversion: Comfortable in inner world of thoughts and ideas
(wait as person interally forms answers)
Extraversion: Focus on outer world
(banter back & forth until arrive at a conclusion of issue being discussed)

CHAPTER 4

The Personality Types in Policing

People are usually attracted to occupations that appeal to their strongest preferences for doing things. As an example, have you ever wondered why accountants, as a group, seem to share some basic personality characteristics with each other, such as an attention to detail, established standards, seldom making errors of fact, and demonstrating a responsive structure and routine to what they do? Another example would be to observe those in the ministry who have an innate and strong concern, warmth, and compassion for others, along with a desire to understand human nature. How about artists, who demonstrate a talent for creativity, inspiration, and sensitivity? If you observed the characteristics of people in many occupations you would see much similarity in personality characteristics and behavior in how they perform their jobs.

Data regarding police personality types indicate 65-70% of law enforcement professionals are Sensing-Thinking (ST), 14% Intuitive-Thinking (NT), 11% Sensing-Feeling (SF), and 6% Intuitive-Feeling (NF) as measured by the Law Enforcement Personality Profile. When comparing personality descriptions with the law enforcement job tasks, the alignment between work environments and preferences indicate clear differences. For example, notice how there are similarities, but also differences:

Type	ST	NT	SF	NF
Process Info	5 senses	6th sense	5 senses	6th sense
Focus on	Logic / Objective Reasoning	Logic / Objective Reasoning	People	People
Prefer work	Structured / Established	Complex challenges	Details / Concrete Reality	Conceptual projects

When making decisions, ST and NT both focus on logic while SF and NF focus on people. Yet, ST and SF are similar in their preference for working in reality of the "here and now", while NT and NF enjoy more abstract, future-oriented projects.

It is important to note that there is nothing inherently bad or good about the 4 personalities. This information was designed to help individuals understand their colleagues and themselves.

The remainder of this chapter explores each of the personality preferences in more detail. Common adjectives associated with the 4 types are included and the common pitfalls for each type reveal situations that may affect their work.

Sensing –Thinking (65-70% of law enforcement)

ST law enforcement professionals prefer to take in and process information through their five senses and then make decisions through pure logic or objective reasoning. This profile comprises the great majority of police officers.

Some words that describe ST officer's behaviors are:

Concrete	Logical	Traditional	Decisive	Thorough
Observant	Practical	Impersonal	Sensible	Pragmatic
Factual	Structured	Direct	Analytical	Service Oriented

These officers are generally extremely good at handling details and can absorb a great number of facts. They like being sequential, taking one step at a time. They enjoy working under a structured plan and like established ways of doing things, such as following a policy and procedure manual. They reach a conclusion through careful analysis and are generally patient with routine tasks. They are seldom wrong with the facts. They are practical and analytical. They are naturally brief and businesslike, and if forced to choose between tact and truthfulness, they will usually choose truthfulness. To others they may appear serious, structured, and very literal.

They like to organize, control, and run things and usually have a natural, logical head for business. Because of their objective and realistic grasp of facts, they can usually do well in other occupations that deal with practical issues and analytical behavior such as banking, applied science, mechanical engineering, production activities, construction, doctors of surgery, and mathematics.

They are not likely to be convinced by anything but reasoning based on solid facts. Appealing to their "feeling side" by using words such as "compassion, caring, sharing, gentleness, or sensitivity" will most likely fall short of the mark.

Possible Challenges for ST's

Job activities of the law enforcement profession seem tailor made for STs. Using the basis of a structured policy or procedure manual to follow, they usually can handle rapidly unfolding, unpredictable chains of events while maintaining their "cool." They can wade right into an extremely complex and personally distressing situation exhibiting a very calm professional exterior.

However, because of this objective reasoning, they may fail to take personal issues of those individuals around them into consideration. They may appear to be blunt and insensitive and neglect basic courtesies that may seem unimportant or a waste of time to them at the time. They also may overlook long-range implications in favor of realistic day-to-day activities.

The STs seem to personify the "tough cop" image. They are what most people in and out of the profession picture when they describe how police officers generally conduct themselves.

Intuitive –Thinking (14% of law enforcement)

NT law enforcement personalities are the second most common in the profession. They prefer to take in information through their "sixth sense" or Intuition and then decide, as STs do, through pure logic and objective reasoning. These officers can be described as:

Precise	Global	Logical	Factual	Goal-Oriented
Detached	Decisive	Strategic	Demanding	Conceptual
Visionary	Reserved	Cognitive	Theoretical	Independent

Since they take in information and process it through their intuition, they look for possibilities and usually do well with complex project activities. They enjoy challenges but may neglect routine tasks. They make decisions like the STs do, so they generally fit into the profession without feeling like an outsider. Because of this decision-making preference, they also will tend to use truth over tact. However, they may appear "scattered and drifty" to STs because of their inattention to detail.

They are the ones that are constantly coming up with new ideas on how to do things and may quickly move from one task to the next without finishing the preceding one. They communicate in global terms, often skipping steps and appearing to talk in circles. They reach conclusions rapidly and are challenged by complex problems. In addition to policing, they can do well in occupations that deal with research, law management, architecture, consulting, and education

They usually dislike detail and routine and may overlook the present while looking toward the future. They may forget specifics, but enjoy being involved in long-range, global activities. Paperwork is not usually their long suit and they can become bored easily.

Possible Challenges for NT's

NTs can be naturally impatient with routine and may fail to focus on practical facts, issues, and details. Because they prefer making decisions with pure logic, they can appear to be blunt and insensitive. They may need to concentrate and focus on one issue, making sure that detail is covered on that issue before moving on to the next. They need to pay attention to people and their concerns. In this profession as in many others, NTs, because of their focus on global issues, tend to seek out job tasks that utilize this preference.

Intuitive Thinking types are often found in supervisory or management positions, not necessarily because they like dealing with people, but because they like to manage complex tasks. In fact, dealing with people problems is not usually one of their favorite things. Because managing and leading people comes with the job of being an administrator, NTs often need to pay special attention to simple personnel issues, such as thanking people for a job well done. In the realistic, impersonal, logical world of law enforcement, NTs can also personify the "tough cop" image.

While NTs and STs are both task-oriented, SF and NFs are feeling-oriented, which is uncommon in law enforcement. The percentage of STs (65-70%) and NTs (14%) compared to SFs (11%) and NFs (6%) in law enforcement is indicative of personality alignment; most SFs and NFs are not drawn to nor do they stay in law enforcement.

Sensing –Feeling (11% of law enforcement)

SF officers comprise only 11% of the profession. Like the ST group, SFs prefer to take in and process information through their five senses, but prefer making decisions with a primary concern for people and the impact of their decisions on them. Some characteristics of these officers are:

Sociable	Caring	Considerate	Practical	Organized
Friendly	Loyal	Trusting	Tactful	Structured
Thorough	Cooperative	Traditional	Observant	Concrete

Like STs, SFs seem to focus on detail and concrete reality. They are practical, observant, and structured. However, since they make decisions through Feeling, they tend to be more aware of and sensitive to people and their feelings while necessary police work decisions are made. SFs seem to do very well in law enforcement tasks of community relations, media relations, personnel matters, and anything where people concerns or relations are paramount. In addition to doing well in law enforcement, SFs can do very well in health care, sales professions, teaching (especially K through 12), supervision, and community and religious service as well.

Because of their people orientation, SFs appear to be different than most other officers in law enforcement. They are best with practical situations that need sound common sense and practical ability in dealing with people. In investigative matters, they are the ones that seem to be able to relate with the "crooks" best and usually seem to have an uncanny ability to cultivate strings of informants and sources on the street. Because of their preference for Sensing, they seem grounded in reality, are thorough, and accurate.

When compared to the 70 percent of Sensing Thinking types found in police work, we can see why the profession does not appear to be a caring, feeling, and compassionate one. Being in the minority of police officers may cause some problems for them, especially with those with little seniority, as they may feel they don't quite fit in.

Possible Challenges for SF's

Law enforcement is generally a pragmatic, structured, impersonal, logical world and most in the profession behave in that manner. Because of their preferred decision-making style that favors people and human values, SFs may not seem sufficiently "tough minded" to the rest of the officers. SFs themselves can notice this difference within a few weeks of entering the force, either as an officer or as a recruit.

If SFs do not understand their own natural strengths and try to act as STs do, they may overcompensate by acting more blunt and insensitive than the STs themselves. It is natural for most people who belong to any professional group to try to fit in and act like the majority act.

SFs have innate strengths that can be an asset to law enforcement and, thus, should not try to "fit in".

SF officers bring a needed, balancing dimension to the field of law enforcement, especially if they find themselves in tasks that involve continual relationships with people. In this new wave of citizen concern, SFs can be excellent community-oriented police officers.

Intuitive –Feeling (6% of law enforcement)

NF officers comprise approximately 6 percent of the law enforcement population and are, like SFs, "uncommon types" in the profession. NFs prefer to process information through Intuition and then decide through Feeling, or social value. Some general descriptors of NFs are:

Global	Gentle	Creative	Idealistic	Compassionate
Committed	Intense	Devoted	Empathetic	Perceptive
Friendly	Diplomatic	Conceptual	Congenial	Charismatic

NFs tend to think globally and enjoy working with people. They excel at long-range issues and conceptual projects. They are responsive to people's needs most of all, showing real concern for what others think and want, and they try to handle situations with due regard for others' feelings. They can usually lead a group discussion with ease and tact, but dislike routine and detail. Being conceptual in nature, they may try to take on too much, not paying attention to detail of projects they've already started.

In law enforcement, NFs are personnel-oriented individuals (e.g., chaplains, employee representatives, psychologists) and can be charismatic leaders. Most enjoy working in juvenile, community relations, and other community-oriented jobs. They also can be excellent at research related activities where an insightful, long-range view is valuable. In addition to law enforcement, their strengths serve them well in behavioral sciences, art and music, religious service, psychology, and teaching, especially at the conceptual university level.

When most NFs enter law enforcement they expect that the majority of the tasks will be to "help people and provide a service to the community." Yet, the profession is dominated with structure, pragmatism, practicality, logic, decisiveness, traditionalism, and by individuals who appear impersonal. The same situation is in any other profession with the same characteristics, such as engineering, banking, mathematics, the military, and physical sciences. NFs may choose to leave, but those that stay bring a compassionate and global perspective to their profession.

Since there are few of this type in law enforcement, they often stand out from the mainstream of officers as being different. This may cause some problems in adjustment, especially with a younger officer. Most of these individuals who start in the profession drop out, feeling that the job was not as they expected it to be.

Possible Challenges for NF's

As with SFs, NFs may not seem sufficiently "tough minded" to most of the ST officers. Like SFs, NFs may find themselves over-compensating as they try to act like the "Thinking types"; they may become insensitive and autocratic, and appear to lack all concern for people. This pull to operate in the Thinking function, which is not their preferred function and is therefore less developed, can be a source of internal and job-related stress. They, as do the SFs, make excellent people-oriented police representatives that can relate to the community well.

Jungian Cognitive Types in the general population:

One way to demonstrate that people select jobs that appeal to their strengths of preference is to look at the distribution of cognitive styles across the US population. According to the Center for Applications of Psychological Type, 1996 estimates reflected 32-42% of the population functioned with the Sensing Thinking cognitive style, 15-22% were the Intuitive Thinking style, 31-41% the Sensing Feeling style, and 15-21% the Intuitive Feeling style. In 2019, 66-74% were Sensing compared to 26-34% Intuitive and 40-50% Thinking compared to 50-60% Feeling. Recent research does tend to reflect these same general distributions.

Researching police behavior and personality using the Jungian cognitive style framework initially began in 1978. Wayne Hanewicz, from Michigan State University, published an article on law enforcement behavior using Jungian theory as measured by the Myers – Briggs Type Instrument® (MBTI). During the 1980s, Ron Cacioppe and Philip Mock from Australia, and Ron Lynch from North Carolina published research on Jungian personality types. In 1991, Hobart M. Henson generated research with the Illinois State Police and Stephen M Hennessy continued with research as late as 2016 that used the Law Enforcement Personality Profile® as well as the MBTI to confirm Jungian cognitive styles as consistent throughout policing ranks. Additionally, an unpublished recent confidential study of over 2,000 police personnel, both sworn and civilian, using the MBTI™ reflected that findings were consistent through the decades with regard those in the policing profession sharing the same cognitive styles.

When reviewing the distribution of personality styles across law enforcement professions, one notices that a very small minority are NFs (those who prefer taking in information through Intuition and making decisions through Feeling). Research on other professions shows almost the reverse, particularly those involved in the helping professions. Most Feeling Types are in professions such as sales, social work, artists, K through 12 teachers, the ministry, psychologists, and those in higher education.

The lack of NFs in law enforcement makes a lot of sense when considering the tasks involved in policing and law enforcement. Tasks are generally structured, finite, somewhat routine or repetitious, and based in present reality. What is and what is not a violation is defined by law. Departments run on rules and regulations with policies and procedures for almost everything. The general description of the job of policing, as well as the function of a law enforcement agency within the community it serves, does not call for an overwhelming need for experimentation, variety, innovation, or creativity. Instead, what is needed is stability, structure, and continuity. The descriptors or general characteristics or behaviors of various police agencies fit the job description.

This is not to say that certain personality types should not be police officers, sheriff's deputies, conservation officers, state police, highway patrol officers, corrections officers, private security officers, or any other occupation involved in enforcing various laws, both civil and criminal. All personality types can be and are very successful in any task they may choose to take on in this profession. Actually, those individuals that comprise personality types that are in the minority in the profession, such as the Feeling types, the NFs specifically, can and do bring refreshing depth and variety to the tasks of policing.

POLICE
AT A GLANCE
PERSONALITIES

SENSING-THINKING

65-70%

Process Info: 5 senses
Handling details
Absorb great # of facts
Working under structured plans
Patient with routine tasks
Practical/Analytical
Brief & Businesslike
Prefer truthfulness over tact

INTUITIVE-THINKING

17%

Process Info: "6th sense"
Look for possibilities
Enjoy challenges (not routines)
Quickly move from task to task
Often skip steps and avoid details
Reach conclusions rapidly
Look to the future
Prefer truthfulness over tact

SENSING-FEELING

11%

Decision concern:
People
People-oriented
Details and concrete reality
Practical / structured
Common sense
Thorough and accurate
Sensitive to feelings
Observant

INTUITIVE-FEELING

6%

Decision concern: Social value
Think globally
Dislike routine & detail
Enjoy conceptual projects & people
Responsive to people's needs
Communication with ease & tact
Can be charismatic

LAW ENFORCEMENT PERSONALITY PROFILE

CHAPTER 5

Choosing Law Enforcement as a Profession

Most individuals assume people pick their occupations carefully. If people are going to spend most of their lives in a profession, shouldn't they concentrate on choosing an occupation that is the best fit? In many cases, people seem to stumble into an occupation which happens to suit them. Yet, consider the time in high school, early twenties, or early college years and there is evidence that people "test" various jobs or tasks. They quickly discard or leave jobs they don't care for or weren't very good at. This "testing" is very subtle in nature, involving our study, our work, and our play. Eventually, for the most part, people find themselves in an occupation which seemed to fit.

In our research we found that most individuals in the policing profession enjoyed it and were good at it. However, very few police executives recalled deliberately choosing law enforcement as the job they always wanted to have. The vast majority seemed to "just find themselves" there.

Entering Law Enforcement: Intuitive-Feeling Types:

All but one of the NFs in this sample did not plan to become police officers. The one officer who planned to enter the occupation was really interested in becoming a game warden, but was too far down on the hiring list. He subsequently was hired by a rural sheriff's department:

> *"Basically, I wanted to help people. At that time, I wanted to conquer the world and help people. My favorite course in rookie school was first aid...I knew it would help me in my job... helping people. When I responded to an accident, I knew I would need to know the stuff."*

Other NFs in the sample came into law enforcement in various ways. One man entered law enforcement between his undergraduate and graduate work. He was playing music at a saloon and got to talking with the deputy that was serving as a bouncer.

> *"I was employed as a guitar player...studying sociology and psychology. I rode around with a deputy friend a bit and I liked it. I thought it was a pretty good deal. When I was sixteen, I would pick up my girlfriend, put a buck's worth of gas in the Volkswagen and go drive down the back roads with the radio on. Now the county buys me a big fancy car with an AM-FM stereo radio with the red lights and sirens and all kinds of toys to play with and air conditioning and I go down the back roads listening to the tunes. I don't have my girlfriend with me but what the hell... they buy the gas".*

Another officer grew up in a lower middle-class neighborhood where he liked and respected the police with whom he came in contact. That was in the days of beat cops on Lake Street and the park police, "...and like I say, generally, they would be very helpful, nurturing, good people. Now if I would had met the bad ones, I might have felt differently..." He met several probation officers because of the nature of the neighborhood and the fact that some of his friends were in trouble with the law:

> *"So that's the way I came into it. I thought this is a good job, this is where you can make a difference in society. Kind of a uniformed social worker I guess is how I looked at it."*

Several other individuals, both now heads of their agencies, never wanted to get into law enforcement. One finished a double major in English and speech communications. Several of his good friends joined the police department as a way to get out of the draft. He had been urged to join as a way of getting out of going into the service, but really wasn't interested in the profession:

> *"I wasn't going to be a cop. I didn't want to be a cop. So I got drafted. I did some AWOL apprehension while I was in the service... That was interesting and when I got out I thought a little bit about law enforcement, but I didn't want it for a career. I wanted to teach in college. My wife's father had been a cop and she told me she had no intention of being married to a cop...she said they drank too much...and always the half priced meals, the free coffee, 10 percent discount at stores, the whole image. So I looked around for a job and while at it, took the Fairfield City police test. They offered me a job... my wife was kind of upset about that, but I said, well it's different, it's a suburban department.*

The head of another large agency majored in business administration and earned a master's degree in Sociology. When asked why he became interested in the profession he replied:

> *"I wasn't. My dad was a cop, my uncles were cops, my cousins were cops and the last thing I wanted to be in the world was a cop. My aptitudes, as I was growing up, leaned more towards writing and history. I was a history major in college until it*

finally sunk in that if I wanted to make a living, I had better switch to something else. And still to this day, I don't know why I became a cop. I care a lot about people and I wanted to help people, I guess..."

Entering Law Enforcement: Sensing-Feeling Types

In the SF group, only two individuals planned to become police officers. One stated, "Well, I determined in the sixth grade that I wanted to be a police officer and I never changed my mind through today." The other said, "I guess I always was interested in police work from the time I was a teenager." The other six SF officers took the job because at the time law enforcement looked attractive:

> *"Originally, I wanted to go in the Catholic seminary. Then I found out ya can't get married. Then I went from there to education ... there wasn't a whole lot of opportunity in education without a high GPA, so I thought I should think about something else."*

He spoke with a friend who was joining the St. Paul Police Department and decided to test for several other departments too. He applied for, and was accepted by, a major metropolitan police department.

Another stated: *"I wasn't really looking for a career, I was just looking for an interesting job and the police department was hiring."*

An SF, who later became the chief of a large police agency, happened to be looking in the paper one day and saw an advertisement for police officers in the help wanted section. Before that, he had never had any desire to be a police officer but had always admired them.

The vast majority of NFs and the SFs did not really plan to become police officers. NFs and SFs used words like "people" and "helping people" in their communication patterns, words that were absent among thinking types.

Entering the Profession:
Intuitive-Thinking Types

Similar to the feeling types, the thinking type officers just seemed to fall into the occupation without a lot of forethought. Of all the NTs, only two felt they had been called to law enforcement occupations.

An NT captain in a major metropolitan law enforcement agency, and a licensed attorney, became interested in law enforcement by chance. He enlisted in the army and picked jump school as a skill choice. He ended up in a military police group, was transferred to Germany, and assigned to a local criminal investigative division. He enjoyed the investigative work, and when he was discharged, went home and took the police test. After joining the department, he was assigned to work midnights on the west side:

> *"I enjoyed the freedom. I always thought of police work as we were 'smarter than' they were. Sometimes it was a matter of trying to be smarter than they were and catch them."*

He went back to school, completed his degree, and then attended law school during the evenings. Shortly after graduating, he was assigned to research and development:

> *"I liked the newness of it. I mean the projects we did. When you got an assignment, you had to create a way not only to get it approved, but to create a way to get it to work. The thing about research...as soon as you think you've got it all together, somebody else points up another problem...and afterwards you just adjust and react and solve them. Some things were unsolvable, there was no solution to them... but a lot of people I work for, or work with, want simple answers to very complex problems and there aren't any, so that was frustrating."*

Another officer, an NT director of a law enforcement agency, "felt a calling" during seventh or eighth grade to become a police officer. He attended college and became a community service officer for a suburban police department. When he became a licensed police officer for the same suburban department:

> *"(I worked) everything from traffic accidents to burglary calls, domestics, emergencies...I couldn't stand to process a crime scene. Just that detail work, the idea of getting there and looking for fingerprints... that was just worthless. But I did enjoy things like traffic... thoroughly enjoyed doing traffic... traffic accidents. I went into school. Medicals and domestics were fun."*

Comments, like those stated, were unusual. More often, individuals assigned to community-facing tasks were not enthusiastic. For instance, a third ring suburban chief of police, an NT, commented about becoming a police officer:

> *"I was with the Vista project, that's Volunteers in Service to America. I was supervising the Vista project for the north and the south sides of Minneapolis. It was an interesting thing and I wanted to do something that was interesting with people."*

He became frustrated with the Vista project, dismissed some of his people, and made some public statements that the project was not serving people as it should. He later admitted, "Well, I ultimately found out that social work in any form wasn't something I was interested in" — a comment that is characteristic of an NT. So, although the NT indicated he "wanted to do something that was interesting with people", his subsequent clarification - about social work - was much more telling. He enjoyed tasks more than people.

Entering the Profession: Sensing-Thinking Types

STs, who comprise the vast majority in law enforcement, also seemed to "fall into" the occupation without a lot of conscious thought. One ST, who rose to a rank of deputy chief stated, "Quite honestly, I was

51

looking for a decent job." Whereas another ST command officer commented on how she became a law enforcement officer:

> *"I have always been attracted to policing. I have always wanted to get involved in the excitement... the fun stuff on the street. I had an uncle that was a cop and I used to listen to stories. I was always action oriented, even in high school. I love running a squad. It's the challenge of doing right."*

Most ST recruits, when asked why they wanted to become police officers, did not reference "folks" or "people." They said things like, "I have been in sales and wanted to get into a profession that helps people" or "This is one where I feel I can make a difference in society and help people." Their social focus was included at the end of their comments, like:

> *"I have always wanted to become a police officer. It is a good job, has great benefits, and it is highly respected. I have been in the Marine Corps up until now, in the signal corps, and now I want to give back to my community."*

Contrast the Thinking type statement with recruits that prefer the Feeling function. Feeling types spoke about people and community as principle to the profession, whereas Thinking types considered the people-aspect as peripheral to police work.

Even though most law enforcement professionals find they are in an occupation they are satisfied with, the process of choosing that occupation appeared to be random. Again, what the clear majority of police unconsciously did was try numerous tasks and quickly discarded those jobs they didn't particularly enjoy doing or didn't do well. There were some officers who may have felt somewhat uncomfortable in the profession, but could, nonetheless, do the job. They didn't particularly like it, but stuck it out and survived for a myriad of reasons including security, pensions, and other benefits. As with the NTs, NFs, and SFs, STs' choice of policing as a profession seemed to be more accidental than intentional.

CHAPTER 6

Differences in Communication

A real difference can be noted between the Thinking types (STs and NTs), who comprise the majority of law enforcement employees and the Feeling types (SFs and NFs), who are the minority. The two groups look at and speak differently of the tasks of policing. During conversations, the Feeling types talked about people constantly, using many colorful descriptions of street characters, and using the word "people" or "persons" many times. The NFs and the SFs often speak of their strong ability to communicate and relate to people on a personal level. The use of the words people, folks, kindness, appreciation, and the like, are common in the conversations with Feeling types.

The Thinking types, both NT and ST, describe things in more literal, general task terms. One ST deputy chief described his staff as "uniforms and clerks." Similarly, an NT captain described his transfers in terms of tasks rather than in terms of people. The STs typically discuss their jobs in the terms of performing tasks rather than the people they encounter while doing them, while NFs and SFs seem to describe their occupations in the context of dealing with violators and describing their associates as individuals.

Dealing with People: The NFs and SFs

While on duty, the primary concern of Intuitive-Feeling types is helping people. Their abilities are strongest in talking with and dealing with people. An NF deputy sheriff commander from a large metro sheriff's office said:

"My favorite calls were domestics. Back then there wasn't any domestic assault law so you just went in there and broke it up... it was kind of fun to go in and defuse the situation. I could talk to just about anybody about anything. I learned to like, and still like, an honest crook, a guy that makes his living being a crook. When you catch him he doesn't give you a lot of baffling bullshit...I mean periodically you run into somebody that there ain't any point to talking to, I then arrest his ass and throw him in jail. End of story."

Another NF commander of a large agency spoke of his early experiences working in a rural area of southern Minnesota:

"Here in the city if you get into trouble you pick up the radio and you get help. My experience in the rural area was the best I ever had...it taught me so much that you have to talk to people. You learn that when a big Dutch farmer is drunk and he tells you he doesn't want to go to jail and to take him home and come pick him up Monday morning and we'll go to court, you can trust him and believe him. Here (in the city) you'd have more of a tendency to slam him up against the trunk and throw the cuffs on him. If you did that down south in farm country at 2:00 a.m. you would probably go home by yourself with your handcuffs in pieces."

To talk himself out of a potentially dangerous situation using a friendly manner was a critical attribute for the job and location. Prior to this same individual being promoted and assigned to his present command, he was transferred to a precinct which had a reputation of the officers getting in fights with violators much more frequently than in the other precincts. He commented on why he felt that was happening:

> *"There's a reason I believe the cops are being assaulted. Here the city's not that bad. We have some tough neighborhoods but any cop who is getting thumped a couple of times a week... there's a reason they are getting thumped... it's because of the way they may be treating people, in my mind. I just told them that it's no longer acceptable to treat people as less than human beings and if you do and you're wrong, I'm going to have your head. On the other hand, I'll stand right next to you if you do your job aggressively and right".*

The commander gave the officers several days of communication training on how to better interact with the public, emphasizing they were there to serve the public. He noted that his complaint level was down almost 40 percent, while the incidence of police injuries was down more than 80 percent.

Working in a rural sheriff's office, one NF lieutenant talked about first coming to the department:

> *"Yeah, I didn't even own a gun, I didn't have a uniform. I borrowed a friend's uniform...the sheriff gave me his gun and holster and said, just don't shoot anybody, just drive around. Don't make any traffic stops unless someone runs into you."*

He particularly liked the domestic calls in the rural areas. They tended to revolve around family problems such as the kid coming home drunk or the disputes between families:

> *"They would say "Go take care of that guy" and I'd roll down there and was able to talk my way through that...I was very comfortable talking and dealing with those folks. I guess I didn't feel I was any better than the folks I was dealing with on the street... the citizens. I could easily see where I could*

be in the same position as they were. You have to find a way to deal with these folks on their level. I didn't write a lot of tickets because I didn't have to. I would walk right up to the kid and say I'm going to be here night after night, and if I see you doing that again I'm going to write you up. That seemed to work for me. I gained a lot of respect from the kids that way. I know there are other, more creative ways of dealing with something other than just a black and white hard-assed police attitude. I always believed in and thought people were individuals, and that every situation was different. So, I look for the difference in people and treat them with what the situation needs."

The police group representing the SF preference obviously shared many of the same social value and warmth considerations as the NF group.

"For example, working in a poor neighborhood with a lot of minority group types, blacks and Indians, poor white people, a lot of welfare folks and stuff I saw my job as really helping and serving and supporting these people. I would ride down the street and spend a lot of time waving at people as I went by and they would return the wave... or to stop at a playground and just talk to some kids in the field and stuff. I was more than willing to get involved in arrests and scuffles if it was necessary but the attitude of cops against the public and the public are the bad guys didn't wash with me. You can't treat people that way."

The next comment also reflects the concern for people or people orientation, as spoken by a Sensing- Feeling commander in a rural sheriff's department:

"The sheriff that originally hired me made the comment that he didn't care if it was a little old lady that had a cat piss on her porch. He wanted her contacted because that was the most,

the single most important thing in her life at that moment.
I think the theory is very good. In law enforcement, it's the
contacts, even though the mediocre calls aren't necessarily
exciting...you take care of them, and I think you gotta keep
that uppermost in your mind... what are the people problems,
and to deal with them."

To this deputy, the important part of the job involved treating
people in an appropriate manner:

"To me that's one of the biggest parts of the job. You gotta
understand the citizen. You gotta have some feeling towards
them and it can't always be negative. Just because they were
going 70 in a 55 does not make them public enemy number
one. Think of the times we personally forget to pay attention
and end up speeding. I see younger officers thinking that the
speeders are bad, totally bad and I have a hard time handling
that. I try to get it across to them that they are just citizens
that we caught speeding. Maybe because of my nature I'm too
far on the other end of the spread, but I'm trying... my goal
is to reach a happy medium."

Another example of general concern for people expressed by
a Sensing-Feeling type comes from an officer with twenty years
seniority:

"I went down and walked the beat near Douglas Avenue,
which was our Black neighborhood. I loved working down
there. One had complete latitude to do any kind of police
work one wanted to and I liked the people and they liked
me. It was a dream for a young policeman. There was all the
police work in the world you could do. And fun type stuff...
Old stuff like go to a crap game in the garage and run in and
scream and watch them all go out the doors and windows and
then you pick up the blanket with the money and dice on it
and then walk down to the little old Black church and say to

the minister, here's a gift from the community for ya. It was real storybook stuff.

"I just liked the people. They were fun. They were energetic, they were also involved in a lot of crime, too. It was a police officer's dream. I just went down there looking at it as a real opportunity to have a lot of fun doing police work and that's just what it ended up being...it was every street character in the world, pimps, whores, junkies, anything you wanted was there, and in those days, the beat officer had a tremendous rapport with these people."

Another Sensing - Feeling officer from the same department was a relatively large, quiet man who really enjoyed his assignment with the juvenile division. He was assigned to that group for several years and was then promoted to lieutenant. He supervised the unit for another year and was then moved to internal affairs. He said his favorite assignment was working juvenile. He really liked working with the kids and would have been content to stay there for the rest of his career. He felt that one had a better chance of making an impact on kids as opposed to working with adults. His time in juvenile was limited though, and he was assigned to internal affairs and then to family violence. The cases he handled there were sex crimes such as rapes, exposures, child abuse, and domestics. He took the transfer to get out of internal affairs because he didn't like the adversarial relationship with his fellow officers but he didn't like the family violence assignment at all:

"It was a depressing place to work. Ya know, constantly han- dling child abuse cases and rapes and all that kind of stuff is hard work... emotionally hard. Ya know when you have to interview little kids about how they were molested by their father or what have you, it's not fun stuff for anybody. I would think my strongest point would be my concern for people. I don't know what term one would use, not necessarily a nego- tiator or counselor or anything like that, but I suppose when

I was a detective I...had an ability to talk heated situations down as opposed to taking physical action right off the bat. Of course sometimes it didn't work and one had to take physical action."

Another lieutenant, an SF from the same department, described his tour of duty in the jail of a major metropolitan department during the 1960s. His affinity for people is quite evident in the following excerpt:

"No...it was horrible, it was like before the industrial revolution. It was a jail...a prison. We had people in there with communicable diseases... we had people in there that were so sick they were dying. I can remember the American Civil Liberties Union came over and forced (them) to come up and examine the jail. The poor guy never wrote a report...I think he went out of there so beat up because I told him...I have to work and live with these people every day. I take chances and give these people major medication to get them through because they are so sick. I give them alcohol, I give them anything to get them going because they are dying on me...I took the inspector back and they were like tiger cages. It was a jail built back in 1890. It had never been updated... it was a horrible year of my life."

Much the same concern for working in and among people exists in the rural areas. One 6 foot 3 inch, 225 pound SF officer stationed in a rural sheriff's office began his career on the sheriff's water patrol. His uncle had been the chief of police in his home town and his father had been a police officer. This SF had been a religion major in college and is now an ordained deacon in his church.

"I didn't care for the serious car accidents... (because of my) feeling for people. When they were hurt and so forth it bothered...I did find it bothered me...And that was something I had to learn... learn to overcome and live with. The contact

with people, I would say for the most part, was good and enjoyable and that's what I enjoyed. Trying to work out and work with them or their various problems. I've had a hard time with some officers who seem to think that it's us against them and view most situations in a black and white manner. Most of the folks we deal with are honest folks and are just in a jam. They need a little consideration too."

STs and NTs and the Tasks of Policing

Sensing Thinkers (STs) and Intuitive Thinkers (NTs) are generally systematic and analytical, often to the point of being or seeming impersonal. As we contrast the descriptions of tasks and duties by SFs and NFs with those by STs and NTs (the majority of cognitive types in the law enforcement profession) one can easily see the difference in concern for people and concern for task.

An example of this orientation is clearly reflected by an NT captain of a major metropolitan agency. He commented on walking a beat. Note that he never mentions people in his description:

"Walking...I kinda preferred that. I had the opportunity several times to ride what they called the district squad in a car and declined. Wanting to work there in the center of the action, so to speak. Something always going on, variety that we always like, and lots of learning in the center setting as opposed to way out in a district in the far end of the city where one just didn't have much exposure to policing activity."

Contrast that description with the following colorful quote from an earlier comment by an SF officer in the same department.

"I just liked the people that lived there (on the beat). They were fun. They were neat; they were energetic; they were also involved in a lot of crime. There was every street character in the world: pimps, whores, junkies...anything you wanted was there."

In a discussion about what they liked about police work, one ST, who eventually became a deputy chief, stated *"I had a lot of freedom. I really enjoyed the variety. One just never knew what the next minute was going to bring. I enjoyed that."*

He further commented on working traffic:

"I almost have to say that I enjoyed sort of the cat and mouse game, trying to catch them doing something - that sort of became a competitive type thing. I really kind of enjoyed, strange as it sounds, taking care of crashes where one can really dig into things and one can...I even liked doing first aid and things after I got through it, ya know, I didn't particularly like picking up dead bodies and stuff like that, but I had a few rewarding experiences by saving a few lives along the way."

Another ST enjoyed the traffic aspect of the job, although for him it was part of a larger fascination with the adventure of police duties. He worked with a state agency where the job was generally traffic-oriented, but, because they were sworn, licensed police officers, they could become involved in any law enforcement violation:

"I liked the action, catching drunks... being on the patrol is a great job even if you didn't like traffic. As a trooper, one's got the ability to roll on anything one wants, I mean, one can help other police departments and when action's over one don't have to do any paperwork. One can go in on armed robberies, kidnappings, or chases, or just anything one hear, ya know, with a scanner. One know what's going on all over the metro area. And the other coppers are always happy to have ya show, ya know, they don't feel that we're stealing their thunder. So it was a good job..."

Another Sensing Thinking type, a deputy chief of a large metropolitan department, again commented on the excitement and variety:

"I started the job and found that it was extremely exciting... it was a huge challenge and the structure of the department was changing...I was offered three or four positions, I stayed in patrol only for a year or so and went to the former tactical squad (power shift) with youngest charger on the department."

He was transferred to a special research project which involved teaching civics classes in the school system. He taught criminal justice studies to ninth grade students. The aim was to try to overcome some of the racial tensions and to stimulate understanding of the criminal justice system. He was then promoted to sergeant and assigned to school liaison:

"I was out at Grant Junior High and Central High School which were inner city schools. It was a challenge. It was like transposing street crime into the schools and obviously had the stabbings and the shootings and the drug problems way back then...again it was very challenging and very exciting."

As one can see from the comments, the focus of the STs and the NTs is generally on the excitement and variety of the job, without any real comments about the people. An ST lieutenant working for a state agency was a water patrol officer, drove an ambulance, worked for a sheriff's department as a desk officer, patrol officer, and jailer, and was hired as a narcotics investigator. He commented on narcotics investigations while working in the section:

"I loved it...the challenge, the role playing, the opportunity to... everything, every situation was different as far as I was concerned. You had to try a different approach or use a different line or use a different role... it was a target type situation or a goal out there one had to achieve. It was never dull. It was never boring. It will always be the highlight of my career... enjoyment wise."

He moved from working undercover to organizing task forces
and working complex drug cases. "It was like putting a novel
together, or pieces of a puzzle... it was really enjoyable." He
then transferred into the training area where he developed
new courses for narcotics training.

As is the case with others sharing a Sensing Thinking preference,
concern with task is evident in the above discussions of police work.
In a long, minute discussion of the various transfers this ST officer
was involved with, the only time people were mentioned was in the
comment "...you knew in your mind that the individual was a violator"

This approach contrasts sharply with the comments by the SF
chief of police in describing his task as working in a poor neighborhood with a lot of minorities. "I saw my job as really helping,
serving and supporting these people and would ride down the street
and spend a lot of time waving at people as I went by. I was always
being accused by my partner of laying the groundwork for running
for mayor."

It's easy to identify differences in communication patterns between
various personality types. The next chapter looks at how these various
types of officers chose law enforcement as a profession.

CHAPTER 7

Leadership Styles and How They May Differ

Leadership and Management: Intuitive-Feeling Style

The typical NF style of management is people-oriented and somewhat reflective in nature. An NF street sergeant in a suburban department characterized his management style as follows:

> *"I think I've sacrificed maybe some short-term performance for a long term relationship where in critical situations you may get performance that you may not have had otherwise. Some people think they should be a hard-nosed supervisor and I think they get begrudging results...if they stay behind somebody and crack the whip. This job relies so much on independent performance that (you don't want them to be) out in a car thinking what a jerk their supervisor is. They (the supervisor) can't be everybody's best friend, but if you take the abrasiveness out of it...you get better performance. That's just my style... that's reinforcing the idea of letting people do their jobs and valuing their input and valuing their talents...so I've*

been luckier than a lot of the other supervisors with what I consider to be high performance people."

His comments contained several elements that were characteristic of NFs. The "sacrificing short term performance" principle reflected the conceptual, future orientation of the Intuitives. It also demonstrated a typical supporting attitude toward people.

Another aspect of this managerial style was the premise that administrative power ought not to be abused. From this perspective, "they don't need a clock watcher, they don't need a baby sitter, and they don't need a slave driver." One NF sergeant really resented his previous supervisor who timed lunch breaks, coffee breaks, and was always hustling on the radio to see if he could catch someone doing something wrong:

"It's January, it's 3:00 in the morning, 20 degrees below zero and you haven't seen a car on the road for two- and one-half hours. I don't care if you sit in a coffee shop for an hour because come July or August you aren't going to get a coffee break at all. And I believe that by the end of the year it's all going to wash out within five minutes, and I'm not going to lose sleep over five minutes and neither are you. And I would rather have you be open, and not try to be hiding things from me when you seriously have a problem. I want you to understand that I'm not being chicken shit and want you to understand that you can come to me first."

An NF police chief of a suburban department described his personal management style as emphasizing the service nature of the police role. He stated that the best cops he had, and "ironically, the ones who also have the best enforcement record," were those who were the most service oriented:

"Well, probably what I should do is send you a copy of our annual goals and you'll see where we are. We are primarily service oriented. Basically, the idea is that my number one goal

is that no one should ever have to call us twice. That means that if they call, we will meet their needs. And I've taken it far enough that if it isn't in our jurisdiction, we will connect them to the right one. We won't send people away saying we can't do that... because once they've reached us they have their link. I think I have a very open department. It's participatory in the sense that everyone has a chance to be heard and participate. I'm not democratic by any means, but if somebody has a good idea and if we adopt it, we let them run with the idea whether they are a patrol officer, sergeant, or whatever."

Describing this same outlook differently, an NF captain in a large metropolitan agency commented, "I'm a people person, that's my strongest asset." In his opinion, he considered a potential decision's implications for the people concerned with the decision, before considering anything else.

This captain experienced a continual struggle with his superiors, whom he felt typified an autocratic management perspective. "To make black and white decisions without considering the people involved, I can't do it, even though it would be easier if I could." He was friendly with the people downtown (his superiors), but noted a distinct lack of people skills in the command. He merely hoped they would leave his precinct alone:

"My people skills give me an extra dimension, but also it gives me more frustration because I'm dealing in a culture that historically does not consider the individual people involved... I've never been able to separate cold fact from the people involved. My philosophy is that we are all adults in an adult situation. You know the rules, you do the job. If you break the rules then I have to do something about it, but I'm not going to sit over you with my thumb. It seems to be working (management style)...I get the results that downtown is looking for. If I didn't get the results, though, I'm sure that management would think it's because I am more people oriented and, in their eyes, not tough enough."

The conversational style of the interviewed NFs used the word "people" often and seemed to be more oriented towards the individual. The same was true for SFs.

Leadership and Management: Sensing-Feeling Style

As was the case with the NF group, the SF group represented their skills in dealing with people as their strongest managerial asset:

"I feel that my approach is, let's find out what the problem is, approach that person, sit down with him or her and give them an opportunity to say what is or isn't. And that's where we (the feeling types) differ, because so many times my sergeants will go out and they'll blow off steam... it creates a real conflict in the department.

Another SF chief of a major suburban metropolitan police department commented:

"You have to be sensitive to people's needs. I believe in a chain of command, but it can shut good ideas down... there was a time when the boss came in and gave orders and the people did what they were told or lost their jobs...that's not a creative atmosphere in which to work...you need an environment where you can make good faith mistakes. If you go out and break the law or something, everything is gonna fall on you, but good faith mistakes you learn from and go on. We don't criticize and we don't punish for good faith mistakes. As an example, two officers stopped to pass on some information, maybe personal business, and when they pulled away, one cut a turn too quickly and wiped out the side of both squad cars. I wrote them a note and said I could see where I could do the same thing myself. They (the cars) are in the shop being repaired. Press on, don't worry about it. Because they didn't plan to do that, they will make sure for the rest of their natural

lives they'll never do that again... why should anybody harp
on the issue. It's not productive. Just put it behind you and
get on. They feel more of a part of the organization... that
the car is a piece of equipment and they as people are more
important. You don't have to beat them up and say "Be sure
and don't damage squad cars." They know."

The emphasis on the people behind the job was evident in the
comments of another SF chief of a large metropolitan police agency:

"As far as a management philosophy, until somebody proves
that they aren't to be trusted, I trust people. The thing is... the
days of autocratic rule are gone... the idea that officers require
extremely close supervision because they might do something
wrong is childish. Unfortunately that does happen, but for
the most part I think there should be an expectation that the
people are dedicated enough...to go out and do it without being
told... we all wear the same uniform, we've all got the same
goals, we might have a different approach to these goals, but
nevertheless we do have the same goals. My weakness is because
I'm accessible, maybe too accessible to people (I've been told)...
you're gonna get some hard lumps as a result of that. I think
that because I try to be tolerant, I think I'm more than kind."

Because of their Feeling preference and orientation toward people
and their concerns, the SFs got along well with other officers who
had the same orientation. SFs recognized that associates appeared
to have the same work philosophy as them. When evaluated, these
individuals were also NFs or SFs:

"In a lot of ways, we have some real differences of opinion too
(speaking about an NF associate). But then again when he
does something, in my own mind I know why he's doing it...I
wanna give him a bad time about being too easy, even though
I know I would probably do the same thing. (Speaking about
a different SF manager and associate) Oh, I can understand,

sometimes I don't agree, but I understand I might have made the same decision because I probably relate too well to where he's coming from."

Similarly, an SF sergeant from a rural police department commented about his associations with a fellow officer sharing the same cognitive style:

"In John and I always have, ya know … John's on a different shift, but we've always been able to communicate well together and I guess when there are certain department situations that come up, we always seem to look at them in the same way … we always seem to have the same perspective."

Law enforcement with an SF orientation tend to get along well with NFs and other SFs. Their focus on people and making decisions that affected people's lives were on the forefront of their thinking processes.

Leadership and Management: Intuitive-Thinking Style

By its very nature, the Judgment function of Thinking is a critical concern in law enforcement. Since NTs are generally impersonal and objective, while being matter-of-fact, they may do well with the reasoning requirements of policing. Focused on more of a "broad picture" perspective, an NT may not necessarily be interested in the details of the job. NTs are usually referred to as being the standard executive type.

When the decision-making functions of Thinking and Feeling are discussed in seminars, many NTs and STs comment "Hey, I have feelings too." Obviously, we all have and express feelings. Thinking versus Feeling is not referencing the lack of having feelings, rather the words describe the way people process information and how individuals speak about people and things. Usually, those who make decisions through the Thinking function comment and speak about things very analytically and pragmatically. As an example, an NT head of a large department said:

> *"I don't like the paperwork. I delegate most of that to my lieutenant. Pretty much it's been pure delegation. One of the things I haven't done is I haven't had a formal staff meeting...I don't wanna waste my time or their time having a staff meeting to say, "Hi, how are ya?" If something comes to my attention, I'll fire it to one of my lieutenants or sergeants and say I expect you to take care of this...I delegate it out and expect it to be done, so I don't do a lot of follow up unless... it wasn't done."*

Another NT from a rural department with ten officers commented about the reason he liked his position:

> *"Autonomy. I like to be in charge. I like to be able to make a difference. I like to be able to see things that need a change and make that change. I need to keep the ideas going and the challenge is much more than coming here day after day."*

Note how the previous executive commented about change, which is an NT's strong suit because of the preference for variety, but never mentioned people or his desire to deal with them.

Typically, the NT command officer preferred to deal with tasks and make decisions with a pragmatic logic and preferred to leave the people issues to someone else.

The appearance of impersonality is also true with STs, who are the majority of the officers in law enforcement. Both the NT and ST styles shared the same Judgment function, that of Thinking, and made decisions using impersonal considerations rather than personal ones (Feeling).

Leadership and Management: Sensing-Thinking Style

The STs, like the NTs, described their strengths in management as related to task management. However, the STs mentioned people more frequently when describing their management style than when describing duties. This made sense; at the time of the interviews, officers' primary duties were to deal with people. Still, STs tended to emphasize roles rather than the people filling them as demonstrated by the following deputy chief's description of his organization:

> *"The people below me still have a direct connection to me and they are my ultimate employees or I'm the ultimate boss. We all... the four captains particularly all have interactions with the deputy chiefs... one controls the money and the transfers... another one has influence on investigations and discipline, and we run a rather open shop here so that they can interact with others."*

Another ST deputy chief was relieved he didn't have to deal with a lot of the "people problems" after a reorganization of duties. He described the reorganization:

> *"I can do the others (people tasks) .... but it's not much fun for me. Responsibility for a lot of other people's actions, ya know, that just wasn't much fun. I was responsible for my own actions, didn't have a lot of subordinates to worry about. I put together a set of goals and objectives and I told the captains to write me a plan."*

Notice his words. The ST manager preferred to deal with tasks and not necessarily with people.

Another Sensing-Thinking deputy chief in charge of administration spoke about his managerial style as tough and forthright. He also had a definite preference for dealing with tasks, not people:

"Well, I never thought of myself as being particularly tactful or diplomatic, but these are some of the things I would hear from my subordinates...he's fair, but hard, he doesn't take any crap and he can see through shallow excuses. You know, if I tell somebody to do it, goddamn it I expect it to be done. Period! I've gotten better at that too. The part I disliked most was dealing with the personnel issues...I have pretty good organizational ability... in budget, planning and training".

During his interview, he suggested that perhaps his present duties involved more use of "diplomacy than they were worth." The deputy chief stated he often went out on the street...calling it "a little R and R." When pulling a shift he said, "I go out to arrest drunks and throw 'em in jail. That's exactly what I do." He remarked that he would go back out on the street "in a heartbeat" if his pay and benefits remained the same.

The Feeling types, SFs and NFs, comprise only 20% of law enforcement officers and are generally people-oriented. NTs and STs, who account for 80%+ of policing, are task-oriented. Mental processing preferences may well serve to explain why law enforcement, as a profession, does not have not a lot of "pats on the back for a job well done". The next chapter spends some time with the feeling types. Like everyone who finds themselves around people that are different, we all have a tendency to react in different ways. These officers, particularly the six percent who are Intuitive-Feeling types, bring interesting dimensions to organizations.

CHAPTER 8

The Feeling Types and How They Differ

One might assume that being a Feeling type in the Thinking world of law enforcement would be difficult and, in many cases, this is very true. Bearing in mind that Feeling types are the minority in the policing occupation, they may feel a little out of place or different from the other officers. Humorously, several officers referred to themselves as "oddballs."

Despite their "oddness" relative to those with which they work, the NF managers all seemed well adjusted. Their comfort in the profession may have been due to their relatively long tenure (18.9 years) and the ranks they held. There was an assumption that many of the NFs, who weren't comfortable, left the police profession years ago due to feeling that they didn't fit in. An example of this phenomenon was a 6 foot 3 inch, 240 pound lieutenant from a rural sheriff's office who commented that his size probably shielded him from potential aggravations and teasing from other officers:

> *"Ya know, I never thought about it, but it probably has come to my aid more than I'm willing to recognize. They think "Well, he might talk soft but he looks like he's able to back it up and handle himself." Even when me and a partner would go to*

domestics, we'd separate the couple and then my partner would want to leave. I was the one that would want to spend a little extra time ya know, just sitting down and trying to reason with them, find out what the deal was and help them out a little bit. My partner would say, Ah come on and let's get some coffee. We'll be back here again later tonight when they go at it again." If I wanted to spend a little extra time, I did, and I really didn't get any guff from my partner about being too soft and come to think of it, not from any other cop either."

Still, being a Feeling type in law enforcement caused some personal pain:

"I would say, if anything, I was more caring, a lot more concerned. I think it caused me more emotional problems for myself because things would get to me. Pain bothered me more, I thought, than the average cop. I would let other people's pain bother me too much. I had an experience back when I was working patrol. I was on for three or four years. I had a double fatal chase. After that I almost quit. I always, I guess, from what other people said, had a lot more patience than other officers did. I could sit and listen more. In fact, to this day even the dispatchers always say... one of them the other day said that I'm always even-keeled and very seldom can you see me get very excited and you seldom see me fly off the handle. I can remember one night some years ago we wrestled some guy out of his house during a domestic... took him to the hospital for his drinking. He wasn't very happy. I went by the hospital to see him several days later. He couldn't believe that I would do that... and he wasn't somebody I knew either."

Another NF deputy sheriff shift supervisor knew he was different from the usual police officer:

"Being different didn't bother me as much as it seemed to bother other people. So they must be the ones that have a problem

with where I stand. I don't have any particular problem with where they stand, I don't wanna stand there, but I'm not going to deny them the right to stand there...so when the new hires come on and ask what the hell's this guy all about, they say, don't worry about him, he isn't gonna bother ya... hey, we have this cigar store Indian in our nice dining hall, but other than that, we still have a nice dining hall, he's a nice Indian, but he's still here".

The same officer, who had a Master of Arts degree in Psychology, commented that the demographics of the department were changing. Formerly, to be hired, an officer had to be from the local area and, in the early days, military veterans were given preference for civil service jobs. Now, however, that was not necessarily the case. The department had grown to over 125 people and was comprised of individuals from all over the state. Many new officers coming onto the force didn't have a military background. The supervisor felt that as the pool of more experienced employees grew larger, his deviation from "true north" became less noticeable. He believed that the more diverse a police officer's background, the more accepting officers were of their colleagues who were different from them (Feeling types).

Another NF captain enjoyed working the road (accidents and all), but disliked arresting people:

"I did learn early in my career that I didn't like to arrest people. I always enjoyed driving fast... it makes the blood run, but I always felt bad in the routine traffic arrests. I wish I could give all those people a warning. The whole time I worked the road I never got over the fact I didn't like arresting people. I've worked the metro, specialized in training, taught defensive tactics, first aid, night stick use, from range officers to whatever...and I still don't like arresting people".

A 6 foot 2 inches tall (230 pounds) Intuitive Feeling captain also commented about his difference as compared to most officers:

"Yes, I was different and it bothered me if somebody made a comment about "how the hell can you be in this job being so soft. I would have punched that guy long before that." (He had been talking and negotiating with a violator long after his colleague would have taken physical action.) Or they would be surprised if I got into a scuffle with someone because they felt that I usually would rather talk than fight. I've been in a shooting incident which came out okay. I ended up lifting weights with the guy who was later convicted of murder. I'm sure that didn't endear me to other officers in my station."

An NF street sergeant with a large suburban law enforcement agency spoke about his approach to dealing with problems:

"A lot of times I would come to the same conclusion as to what course of action to take in a given situation, but I think I took greater pains to smooth a situation over a little bit. When you had to tell a citizen or somebody that they were under arrest...I tried to not make it a personal thing between myself and a suspect or something...like some officers feel that the suspect offended them personally so they are going to jail. I have always had a fairly aggressive enforcement stance...I don't apologize for people going to jail or arresting someone, but I have always made a strong effort to keep people satisfied. I want them to know that I'm not judging them personally, but judging what they have done and that's why they are in the position they are in. I've probably spent more time, maybe more time than I should have sometimes, hanging around to talk to people and tell them what we did or didn't do."

SFs recognized they were somewhat different than most of the other police officers in the way they dealt with people. As an example, this Sensing Feeling officer stated:

"I tended to pick partners that were similar to myself Ya know oftentimes we handled, ya know, we always worked as a pair,

and I wouldn't have picked a partner that would go blasting right in a place and start punching people out, I mean that is not my style."

Interestingly, he said he was the exception when first starting police work twenty years ago (late 1960s), but was not necessarily the exception now. He felt the concern for people, their basic rights and dignity, were more important now than years ago:

"I think law enforcement is changing. I think the make-up of the police department was quite different. More females, more diversified work force...higher education level..."

Regarding the changing composition of police departments, an NF sheriff's deputy said the same thing. Hiring a more diverse police force was having a positive impact on the organization.

An SF deputy chief of a large metropolitan agency commented that he was highly enforcement-oriented with "... the highest misdemeanor arrest rating in the station for the four years I was on a power shift." He characterized himself as 'highly enforcement oriented', but wanted to deal with "satisfied customers":

"You can arrest the husband and father for domestic abuse or whatever it happens to be, but you are still dealing with the wife and you're still dealing with the kids and you are leaving the image of the department there. And I was always sensitive to that...I worked with some older guys that didn't necessarily have a high regard for enforcement... carried candy and stuff to give to kids on domestics and I was always touched by that kind of involvement. You are serving those folks and you've got to be selling yourself... always."

Another Sensing Feeling captain from a large metro agency characterized himself as being different from the other officers in his department. At rookie school he was quiet and reserved.

"I didn't fit into the military academy thing at all. I had to get out on my own. I didn't like that regimentation. (When asked if he felt others perceived him as being "soft") …No, not all of the time. I can be pretty miserable if I have to be. I don't like to, but I can. I used to have a real quick temper."

An SF sergeant, stationed in a rural sheriff's office, commented that he didn't think much about being different from other officers for the first part of his career because he worked alone most of the time. When he thought about the question he commented: "Ah… with probably the majority of law enforcement officers, I've been told that I carry my feelings out on my sleeve too much."

And a rather outspoken SF lieutenant from a large metropolitan agency characterized himself as "feeling differently" than most other officers:

"I'm much more friendly with people than most cops. I enjoy people. I like dealing with people. I like talking with people."

Individuals who were identified as Feeling had a genuine appreciation of people. Even if they were enforcement-focused, the Feeling officer considered people before tasks. Decisions were made while considering how those decisions would impact and affect others.

What Happens with Most of Those Who Feel "Different"

When someone entered the police profession, or any profession, and felt "out of place," the person often left. Individuals gravitated towards employment where they felt most comfortable. Yet, there were individuals who stayed who weren't like their colleagues. This was the case in a police training class conducted at a technical college in Minnesota.

In Minnesota, if individuals wanted to become a law enforcement officer, they were required to first attend a two year program at a technical college, university, or community college. After successful completion of the program, individuals completed a 10-week skills course. Upon passing the program and skills course, candidates were then eligible to be licensed upon hire by an agency. Along with a series of other assessment instruments and tests, students in the law enforcement class were given the Law Enforcement Personality Profile®.

The class distribution of profiles was similar to existing law enforcement demographics. Cognitive Judgment styles of Thinking accounted for 80% of the class and 20% were identified as having a Feeling profile. New recruits had the same general Jungian cognitive distribution as Veteran police officers with twenty years on the job!

Contrary to Jung, some sociological theories in the 1960s and 1970s suggested that police personalities were the direct result of the influence of veteran cops on rookie cops. Many sociologists felt that if law enforcement agencies specifically recruited warm, feeling, and compassionate individuals, the police services would become warmer and more compassionate. Yet, the profile results from the Minnesota study indicated that warm, nurturing, compassionate individuals would not be attracted to the profession due to the nature of the tasks required for performing in the profession. Individuals whose attributes were practical, logical, direct, rational, fair, just, structured, and matter-of-fact were attracted to tasks of the occupation. The distribution indicated that rookie cops were not socialized into becoming <u>less</u> compassionate cops. Furthermore, after being on the job for a period of time, Feeling law enforcement officers had <u>not changed</u> their perception or judgment preferences.

An interesting longitudinal note about the law enforcement classes: Half of the Feeling types left the program before their two-year graduation. Most cited "incompatibility" with the program. This feedback seemed to reinforce the issue - people were attracted to jobs in which they could use their strengths. As a cross check, we administered the instrument to two more successive classes and for several years. The distribution remained the same as that of veteran police forces.

Images of law enforcement tended to portray officers as being authoritarian, cold, condescending, and serious acting. The public impression of cops was explained through attribute and task alignment. The stereotypical perception of law enforcement appeared to be a result of mental processing preferences, which Jung felt were present at birth or shortly thereafter. Individuals who had attributes aligned with the job tasks were attracted to the law enforcement profession more than individuals who did not have such alignment.

Physical Size May Affect Success for Feeling Types

The law enforcement profession remains a primarily masculine profession characterized by the rough and tumble, physical situations that the media portrays. Fighting, chases, shootings, struggles, and macho images are continually portrayed in TV and movies. Interestingly, all but one of the Intuitive Feeling types interviewed was at least 6 feet tall and all weighed at least 200 pounds. One exception - 5 foot 10 and one-half inches - lifted weights and was noticeably muscular. The large, imposing physical size of these officers was a disparate contrast to their empathy. Although they may have felt a "deviation from true north" by displaying compassion, they were not challenged by others, which might have occurred had they been smaller in stature.

Feeling type officers realized that they were different from the clear majority of other police officers and decided that law enforcement wasn't for them. A smaller, male police officer with a Feeling decision preference could have been intimidated by other officers through kidding, cajoling, or teasing. This was not necessarily true for female police officers, who were typically smaller in stature than their male counterparts. In fact, precisely because they were women, male officers expected compassion from them. The gendered, cultural norms prevented them from extensive teasing, unlike male officers.

Being a Feeling type in law enforcement may be a self-fulfilling prophecy in regards to job tenure. Many Feeling types tended to be uncomfortable and left for another occupation, which meant there are more Thinking types represented. But the critical issue was the few remaining Feeling types who desired to remain, for whatever reason. Feeling types gave the occupation an interesting depth.

The reverse could be true for the helping professions, including social workers and probation personnel. In these professions, which are dominated by Feeling types, the majority of decisions tend to be made through social value considerations. A person with an impersonal, basic, practical, matter-of-fact, Thinking function might feel uncomfortable with a group of people that are continually expressing compassion, human concern, and are gentle, sensitive, and caring. Both, naturally, want to associate with groups of individuals more like themselves.

Our focus identified how the tasks involved in the policing profession appealed to Thinking types. Many of those tasks were structured, sometimes cold, generally impersonal, logical, objective, and matter-of-fact. If the public desired warmer, nurturing, caring, feeling police agencies that demonstrated compassion, we must first understand the limitations of such a goal. The very nature and structure of law enforcement may make such a change impossible. Most individuals in law enforcement will not "naturally" be people oriented. While we may, and really should, teach officers to be more people-oriented, tasks in policing and their attraction to the Thinking types remain unchanged.

CHAPTER 9

A Brief Look at Females in Policing

Women have been a part of law enforcement for many years, but only during the mid to late 1970's were they finally allowed to function as full-fledged police officers on the street doing the same tasks as male officers. Conventional wisdom deemed women to be physically weaker than men and the street was perceived as too tough for women. Prior to street assignments women were placed in areas where administrators stereotypically felt females would do best, like the records sections, juvenile bureau, or sex crimes. Many women were not allowed to wear uniform trousers but mandated to wear skirts and nylons or hose ... in 100 degree days! They could only carry weapons in their purses, not in a holster on their hip. Many believed women were naturally compassionate. Thus, women could best use their innate sensitivity with sexual assaults and juvenile cases, but policing was a man's profession according to the wisdom of the day.

Research indicates most females tend to be weaker in upper body strength than males. Due to this physical difference, women did not resort to physical force as often as men. To be fair, few calls really require the use of brute force; in most cases, there are several cars as backups at scenes. Regardless, numerous studies found female officers had fewer brutality complaints against them than male officers.

Additionally, various self-defense skills used by both men and women can make up for lack of upper body strength.

Some sociologists have felt that an increase in female police officers on a force may increase police "sensitivity" toward citizens. Some women police officers disagree with such comments, as they don't want to be seen as "weaker" than men. It is generally true, however, and many studies indicate, that women do possess better communication skills than men overall. Many women can use this ability as an alternative to the use of physical force. Women have been part of the mainstream patrol and administrative duties of various law enforcement agencies for years now, and female police officers do as well on the street as males do.

The MBTI and Female Officers

At a seminar on police personalities, we had the opportunity to administer the Myers Briggs Type Indicator™ (MBTI) to 82 female police officers. The MBTI is another well-known cognitive measure resembling the Law Enforcement Personality Profile®. More than 500 women attended the 1990 International Association of Women Police (IAWP) conference in St. Paul, Minnesota. The seminar took place on a Thursday, four days into the conference. Prior to taking the instrument, these female police officers were urged several times to answer the questions as they truly felt they personally preferred, not as they felt their law enforcement occupation or specific organizations expected them to be.

The results of the cognitive measure resembled findings similar to the general population; overall, female police officers had the same frequency distribution as one would expect to find among the population. The percentage of Sensing-Thinking types was higher when compared to the population, but the Sensing-Feeling and Intuitive-Feeling cognitive styles resembled the general population. The SF and ST preferences comprised the majority of female officers, which makes sense in that the occupation calls for Sensing strengths. Interestingly, NF and SF profiles - the Feeling function - accounted for 45.2% of the group. This is a very different makeup than the percent of male officers who preferred the Feeling function (17%) for making decisions.

Female Police Officers
International Association of Women Police Conference
N = 82

Cognitive Style	Abbr.	Percent	Number (n)
Intuitive-Feeling	NF	20.8	17
Sensing-Feeling	SF	24.4	20
Intuitive-Thinking	NT	17.0	14
Sensing-Thinking	ST	37.8	31
Total		100	82

For the law enforcement profession, the Sensing-Thinking and the Intuitive-Feeling preferences were greatly under-represented. For the group of female police officers, their results resembled, and were more aligned with, the general population.

Female police officers accounted for 12 to 15 percent of the total number of officers nationally. Within our studies, some departments only had one female in their sworn ranks. Despite women being under-represented in police forces overall, cognitive type preferences for female officers reflected the general population, and not that of a typical group of male police officers. The majority of male police officers were Sensing-Thinking or Intuitive-Thinking. The majority of female officers were Sensing-Thinking or Sensing-Feeling.

Females in the police profession tended to reflect those behaviors they felt were expected and valued in the profession rather than their "true" type. In other studies, women mentioned how they tried to act like the men to fit in at their departments. Most found, however, that modifying their behavior into what they thought was expected didn't work well. Divergent expectations, like clashes between how a person felt versus cultural attitudes, occurred within Thinking-Feeling.

As a side note, the Profile was administered to Singapore Airlines Police officers, a private police group for the airline. The organization had as many female officers as male officers. Approximately half of the female officers had a Feeling cognitive profile. To identify any on-the-job differences, we would have liked to have spent some time watching them at work. Unfortunately, we were not afforded the opportunity because of time constraints.

Within American culture, feelings, compassion, and warmth were often considered feminine attributes; masculinity was often equated with cold, hard logic and rationality. These stereotypes influenced personal perceptions, which may or may not have aligned with cultural norms. In the case of police tasks and general attitude, compassion and social value were not necessarily appreciated or expected within the profession. While men and women performed the tasks of policing, the research showed they approached the tasks through different methodologies.

The results from the conference may also have been influenced by the environment. Being in a group of female police may have reduced the peer pressure to act as most male officers would act. A casual, relaxed setting may have produced more valid statements regarding personality and behavior, particularly after being coached several times to answer questions in a personal rather than an occupational way. A five day conference with 500 female police officers could also have created a supportive group cohesion; sharing law enforcement experiences common only to women and feeling more validated could have contributed to a more realistic picture of how women law enforcement officers actually function on the job. Regardless, there was intense peer pressure to "conform to the majority", which remained true for the law enforcement occupation.

The issues confronting females in law enforcement were different from male police officers' issues. The conference was an opportunity to address issues specific to their gender. For instance:

- During the 1990s in Minnesota, of the students who entered college with the expressed intent of becoming a police officer, twenty-five percent were women. Among graduating students who intended to go into law enforcement, only five percent were women. Women began their training and initially considered the profession from one perspective and then, as the tasks of the job became more concrete, their perspective shifted and they left the job pipeline.

- Women tended to bring more personal value and compassion to the profession, but decided the profession was not for them after being surrounded by Sensing-Thinking types during their educational journey. Since a Feeling approach to problems was different from a Thinking approach, they could have decided the profession was not the right fit.

Future considerations, especially if the nature of the job of policing changes, included:

- Would policing appeal to more SFs and NFs? Would Feeling types be attracted to the profession?
- Would law enforcement change if there was more concern for human issues? Would the value of individuals change if the profession viewed people in a different light?
- As the dominance of STs and NTs diminishes, would policing attract and retain more Feeling types because their comfort levels increased?
- In regards to Jungian typology and cognitive styles, would the policing occupation resemble the general population? If more women became part of the occupation and stayed, what would be the distribution and frequency of mental processing preferences?

During our IAWP conference presentation, we asked attendees their opinion about what personality and behavior attributes were important for being a police officer. In ranked order:

1. Ability to communicate
2. Ability to make a quick, sound decision
3. Need for compassion.

Public complaints, especially in recent years, have addressed the lack of compassion among law enforcement. The results of this informal survey from the 1990s remain important considerations for 21st century policing.

CHAPTER 10

Potential Challenges of Differing Styles

Different cognitive styles bring strengths to the profession. Using Jungian cognitive styles to provide an understanding of police personalities enables new insights into how people perform on the job. Along with strengths are the weaknesses or pitfalls of the various styles. Taking in information and making decisions can have an effect on performance. Usually, when people become aware of their strengths and weaknesses, and how both affect their performance on the job, they work to deal with both better.

Potential Challenges for Intuitive-Feeling Types

Growth for Intuitive-Feeling types was different from Sensing-Thinking weaknesses. Critiques of individuals with an NF function preference included perceptions that they may:

- not be seen as sufficiently tough- minded to Sensing and Intuitive Thinkers;
- try to please too many people at the same time or appear "drifty" or scattered;

- need to pay more attention to the details of the task and to the concerns of people.

As an example, an NF chief of a large agency recognized that being different from others left him politically vulnerable. Colleagues told him that he was too humane, "You're going to get hurt. You're letting your feelings interfere with your operation." To address areas in need of development, NFs considered the larger implications on their career.

Another Intuitive-Feeling type, a chief of a large metropolitan agency, was aware of police personality and Jungian Cognitive Styles. He purposefully appointed an individual that he knew was good at detail (an ST) to "handle the details." He conceptualized what needed to be done and asked his assistant to fill in the blanks and make it work. He knew his strengths were not in handling the details and that he would not do as good a job as an ST. The tasks were handled well as a result of their teaming together and strategically using their strengths.

Two NF individuals struggled when switching from the street to management because of their concern for the feelings and friendship of others. One characterized the transition as follows:

> "When I became a supervisor, I guess I didn't know how to handle that. I felt that staying in that character of being one of the guys didn't work out because a lot of the guys didn't respect that, they didn't work for me, they didn't do their job, they thought that what the hell, this guy is…well you know, so I came on a bit too strong and too severe and that wasn't supported by the department so I've been spending the last few years backing way off and trying to be more understanding…I tend now to be a little too nice."

He felt more comfortable being a "bit more friendly, and warmer. Sometimes you lose who the hell you are in trying to be someone that you are not." Simply put, his concern for people hindered his managerial roles and he had to find balance between his cognitive preferences and the job demands.

Type dynamics explain why some Feeling types tend to become "hard-assed" supervisors. An NF personality type has Intuition or Feeling as the dominant and auxiliary functions, with Thinking and Sensing as tertiary or inferior functions. Individuals with strong social value (Feeling) preferences but whose job tasks are primarily Sensing and Thinking, like law enforcement, try to emulate ST traits and overcompensate. Individuals often have difficulty being someone that they are not, which results in a more strict interpretation of personal behavior. They deny their feelings and concerns for people in an attempt to act like the managers around them. This dissonance results in an autocratic and hard approach, because they deem their "natural tendency" as inappropriate for individuals in a police occupation.

When Jungian personality theory was explained to police managers, tears formed in the eyes of two NF individuals. Both administrators characterized themselves as "hatchet men" at work. They pushed their concern for people aside under the belief that concern for others didn't belong in management, particularly in management of paramilitary organizations like law enforcement agencies. Understanding the tasks and activities required to perform in a profession becomes extremely important for success.

Jungian personality theory posits that people are born predisposed to prefer some functions over others. A person with a naturally developed Sensing function is assumed to be an astute observer of their immediate environment. With attention directed to the environment, the person spends less time using the opposite function (Intuition). When individuals do not use their natural strengths in their job, the profession or tasks become less satisfying. With law enforcement attracting primarily Thinking preference types, officers with a Feeling function may overcompensate. In trying to balance the use of pure logic (Thinking) with social value (Feeling) these individuals become dictatorial and autocratic. Tasks and activities foster the development of preferences or force the use of weaker preferences.

This personality dilemma seems especially prevalent in occupations like law enforcement. Generally speaking, law enforcement attracts primarily STs. When NFs become cops, they either try to fit in by copying others and their actions, or try to adjust by just accepting their differences. Many cannot adjust and decide to leave because they "just didn't fit in." Others become frustrated and feel they are not being "true to themselves" when they try to act in non-strength areas. Acting like someone else is difficult. Individuals may pretend for a while, but the amount of effort results in generalized exhaustion and/or neurosis over a period of time.

The potential problems, of being with those that don't act like you, applies equally to the other types. If Sensing-Thinking individuals found themselves "trapped" in a warm, nurturing, unstructured environment, they are likely to be extremely uncomfortable. An Intuitive-Feeling supervisor would likely smile, chat, hug, give a pat on the back, and/or be concerned for the employee's welfare. ST employees prefer a structured, realistic, practical, systematic, and concrete task-oriented organization, including consistent and systematic rules. Faced with a more free-flowing and affable environment the ST person may feel as if they are working in a chaotic or disorganized workplace.

An excellent example of imbalance, or "trying to act in a different way than is natural," was noted by an Intuitive Feeling commander assigned to a Southern precinct. He had a reputation of being strict, "too strict by today's standards." To him it was "my way or no way":

> "To tell you, I damn near quit in the first two or three months. I decided this stuff wasn't for me (supervision). I felt like a fish out of water. I felt uncomfortable supervising guys that had three times the time I had on the force. I had some times that I went nose to nose with some guys and I hadn't backed down and I stumbled a few times. I had my boss tell me to lighten up a little bit. Some of the guys perceived me as maybe a pushover. I took a survey a couple times a year on how I was doing... one thing that used to come up pretty frequently was the hard line I took on (my) people".

The commander acknowledged that being a supervisor was hard on him. As a result, even though he had chances for several additional promotions, he turned them all down. He was looking forward to retiring and doing something other than law enforcement.

Potential Challenges for Sensing-Feeling Types

Even though SF officers make decisions based on Feeling they possess a strong reliance on Sensing, which is why they fit into the profession as well as they do. The Sensing grounds them in concrete issues and interactions. The pitfalls for SFs resemble the issues the Intuitive Feeling types deal with, because they may:

- not be seen as being sufficiently tough-minded (the same problem as NFs);
- need to consider global issues, not just present considerations;
- attempt to avoid conflict because of their feelings for people.

One SF commented about being too soft, and recognized this characteristic was making him politically vulnerable. The other police manager said, "You're too humane, you're gonna get hurt. You are letting your feelings interfere with your operation."

SFs had a pronounced job focus, which also occurs for most STs regardless of occupation. Typically, SFs in policing do not report many outside interests other than those around law enforcement. They had fewer dramatic role changes than others and focused on doing their jobs well. They did not necessarily look for lateral or upward transfers, but sought ways to perform jobs with excellence.

Potential Challenges for Sensing-Thinking Types

A beat cop's activities seem perfectly suited to the inclinations of an ST. The rapid, unpredictable chains of events on the street require officers to maintain their "cool". Possible weaknesses for Sensing-Thinking types are they may:

- neglect important personal issues, because they concentrate on pure objectivity;
- overlook long-range implications for day-to-day activities, because they enjoy and tolerate routine well;
- appear blunt and insensitive to those that they work with and to members of the community.

Of the ST managers interviewed, several commented that they didn't like to deal with personnel problems. One ST was relieved when a personnel function was reassigned from him to someone else. None of the STs felt they were different from the majority of other police officers. Some STs asked if they *should* feel differently from other police officers. In contrast to the NF, who described himself as a "deviation from true north," STs often personify the "tough cop." Most people, in and out of the profession, refer to the tough cop stereotype as the "true north" barometer for how cops conduct themselves.

STs enjoyed and felt comfortable within the police culture's emphasis on impersonal, logical interactions. They seemed to sense that they fit in. Some yearned for the opportunity to return to a role where the "true north" style of behavior was preferred. This was especially true if placed in a position that required a personal, warm and human approach.

Potential Challenges for Intuitive-Thinking Types

Like their ST counterparts, NTs also personified the "tough cop" portrayal and were referred to as "true norths" in the profession. The Intuitive function provided the faculties for insight, making rapid connections, and seeing the long-range implications of their actions and of police policies. Pitfalls for the NT function preference included:

- An NT may be too impersonal and unappreciative of input from others;
- They may become forgetful of current realities;
- They could find it hard to focus on practical details and have a problem carrying issues through to the end.

In regards to attention to detail, one NT stated that he was not good at remembering names, license plates, or details of a homicide. Another commented that his partner was "driving him crazy with constant detail." An example of detail inattention occurred with an NT manager of a police academy. A 12 noon meeting was called with five ST subordinates to discuss instructional issues. The STs became irritated as the meeting progressed, with the NT manager explaining that the length of the meeting was sent in the memo. The STs protested that no time length was included, no location for the meeting was stated, nor were they informed to cancel their classes for the meeting. Upon retrieval and re-reading of the memorandum the NT manager realized he had neglected to mention the expected length of the meeting, the subject matter, and where the meeting was to be held. He mentioned that he had "just assumed" he had furnished all of the details to the others.

Interestingly, none of the NTs commented on being too tough or not appreciating people enough. NTs made decisions with pure logic, like STs, and generally did not think that they may not appreciate people. Like most people, they did not have insight to see whether their perception was true. In the context of work, which was grounded in the realistic, impersonal, and logical world of law enforcement, there was not a focus on self-realization. While many NTs in law enforcement acted impersonally, they did not believe that they were impersonal.

CHAPTER 11

Police and Conflicts with Other Professions

A long history of misunderstandings and communication conflicts has occurred between social workers, "newsies", "shrinks", and cops. The methodology behind how each profession does their job contributes to the friction. The professions describe each other in less than glowing terms: "Jack booted, Racist, Nazi cops" or "bleeding heart liberals". The different professions regard each other in less than understanding ways.

Ask any group of police officers to raise their hands if they worked on a case or an incident and read about it the next day in the paper. Then ask if the story was unrecognizable as their case and the hands stay up. While every reporter may not write correctly about an incident, there remains a misunderstanding and conflict between the professions. Police request details be withheld from a story and the newsies publish the information or the newspaper account lacks the details that police think are necessary to tell the full story.

Not every social worker deals with juvenile divisions, but social workers and caseworkers in corrections often feel police lack compassion. They hear the side of the story from the arrestee and allege mistreatment or lack of consideration. Victims' Rights activists are often critical of the impersonal style of many police officers during domestic violence cases. They see a person in crisis, who may be acting emotional and hysterical, and the general response is "in walks a male in uniform with an attitude." The victim may have had months or years of abuse that led up to the situation, but social workers focus on the lack of consideration by an officer.

Each occupation's objectives are different and should be considered to truly understand the disconnect between profession occupation. The assumption that all of the jobs deal with criminal justice, even if the jobs are different, provides a limited understanding. So what could be the difference that makes people in these occupations look at issues in a way different than law enforcement?

The Center for the Application of Psychological Type (CAPT), located in Gainesville, Florida is a repository for years of research using the Myers Briggs Type Instrument®. The assessment measures Jungian Cognitive styles across many professions. Considering various occupations through Myers-Briggs cognitive styles provides information to explain why these inherent differences exist.

The CAPT data bank reflects a sample of editors and reporters, along with a sample of social workers, as having predominant cognitive styles of Intuitive Feeling (NF). The predominant cognitive style among law enforcement is Sensing Thinking (ST), while the least represented style is Intuitive Feeling (NF). The majority (42 percent) of this sample of editors and reporters shows a preference for Intuitive Feeling, while in the police sample, the Intuitive Feeling types were only 6.3 percent. No wonder both occupations look at things differently; there is a vast difference in the way people in the professions look at the issues.

Consider a scenario that police frequently encounter. A police investigator picks up the morning newspaper and reads about a case he has worked on the day before ... and the information is incorrect. Several reasons exist for the lack of information or alignment between what occurred and what was reported. The officer couldn't provide the information to the reporter, or was unable to get a copy of the report to the reporter, or the reporter chose which facts to include and what to omit. The reporter, being global in perspective (Intuitive), may determine the facts are "in the ballpark" which, in the reporter's perception, is "close enough." However, the officer approaches the incident through a Sensing preference, knows the intimate details of the case, and considers the broad generalities as errors in the story.

The police officer, whose Sensing enables him to perceive in great detail, struggles to understand why the reporter didn't say "at precisely 10:32 a.m., the victim descended the stairs and was accosted by the perpetrator ..." and describes the actions that occurred. These details only concern the Perceptive part of the issue. The Judgment side, the decision-making part of cognition, also contributes to the construction of two completely different perspectives.

The police investigator may be dealing with the aftermath of the incident, trying to wash the blood off of his or her hands from the crime scene. Meanwhile, the reporter writes about the assailant and how he was raised in a broken home by an alcoholic single parent who is really sorry that the child got into trouble. The human element is reported, including how the perpetrator really didn't commit the crime, and the police must have beaten a confession out of the assailant. Of course, the story the reporter is writing is a legitimate human-interest story that readers are interested in.

The police officer is looking at the issue through the pragmatic, objective lens (Thinking). He logically thinks the crook should be on his way to jail or punished, not out on the street on bail. The reporter, who makes decisions based on the Feeling function, views the case with social value (Feeling). The human side of the assailant, the family, the spouse, friends, and neighbors are all considered alongside the fate of the victim.

This scenario may be exaggerated somewhat, but illustrates how people generally look at things. Real differences in perception exist. The Jungian Cognitive Styles provides an informed perspective for understanding how people view the world using a mentally cognitive perspective.

Social Workers

The dissimilarity between news reporters and police holds true for social workers. Police and social workers often find themselves on opposite sides of an issue. We are not making a judgment on who is "right or wrong" on an issue, but merely stating that our perspectives will cognitively, be somewhat different. No two people will view an issue through an exactly similar lens; we all tend to see things from our own perspective.

For social workers, the Feeling function preference is over 64 percent. A majority of social workers prefer making decisions based on social value rather than pure logic. Taking the tasks of their occupation into consideration, the conclusion appears appropriate. An example of the mismatch between preferences is provided by Dr. Hennessy.

Dr. Hennessy and the Social Workers

During his law enforcement career, Dr. Hennessy served in a narcotics enforcement section during the early 1970s. One of his duties was training various other governmental agencies on drug identification, drug laws, and investigations. When he spoke with local and state representatives of social service departments, Dr. Hennessy was often treated like an overzealous drug enforcement officer. Some social workers even waited stoically until the question and answer period, then would gleefully ask if he enjoyed putting "poor little teenagers who were just smoking a little weed" in jail. The audience seemed to enjoy discussing the philosophy of punishment and incarceration versus treatment. Hennessy was somewhat challenged around individuals who seemed not to really understand his view; law enforcement was important for drug culture problems. The social workers were equally challenged with him as an objective, structured, law enforcement representative.

Prior to leaving the department of public safety, Dr. Hennessy had occasion to work with a state level social service department. A preliminary study, to improve the state's computer systems for dealing with battered women and domestic violence, was set to launch and Dr. Hennessy travelled the state meeting with various social department administrators. As Hennessy spoke with them, they discussed the operations of civil divisions in sheriffs' departments. One of the managers made an unsolicited statement about how he disliked "police types" because of their apparent insensitivity. The manager's partner, who was listening to the conversation over the office divider, chimed in with several additional negative comments about police officers. As he listened to their comments about police insensitivity, they had not realized they were talking with a law enforcement administrator, not a program and computer researcher, and Dr. Hennessy chuckled to himself at the irony of the situation.

Why the Conflict

Naturally, people feel most comfortable with people they can understand, communicate well with, and who have similar values. Individuals are typically uncomfortable with situations that do not have those kindred elements. Understanding each other's point of view becomes treacherous and difficult. The lack of trust combined with a historical precedent of contention leads to schisms and conflict.

Individuals in law enforcement may feel people in the helping occupations are too soft, unrealistic, fuzzy headed, and too liberal. The following is often surmised:

- Even though a person is deemed innocent until proven guilty, we know the guilty are often arrested.
- The world is full of unprincipled, lying, cheating, stealing low-lives
- Social workers, probation officers, defense lawyers, and psychologists are trying to get degenerates back out on the street faster than police can bring them in.

Likewise, the media's point of view may not make a lot of sense to law enforcement. Reporters make decisions via Feeling - warm, human insight. Law enforcement approaches problems using logical, rational reasoning. It is no wonder that law enforcement personnel are described as cold, hardhearted, non-compassionate human beings. However, neither perspective is wrong; both focus on what they feel is best for the people involved in a situation.

Understanding the multiplicity of people's personality types, and the varied ways they approach a problem, provides insight for why people look at issues the way they do. Jungian typology also gives us a terminology or common verbiage for communication, which we can apply to the different personality types. We can use this vernacular as a tool to understand the different ways we all make decisions, as well as why we make those decisions (different reasons and directions). Many law enforcement officers have had career experiences with the helping professions. With the mental processing preferences, we now understand why different professions seem to look at issues in a completely different light than policing views them. We can better understand each other's points of view and work more as a team in the criminal justice area if all sides are aware of the differences in perception and judgment.

CHAPTER 12

Noticing Types at Work

During our many years in the law enforcement profession, we have had an incredible number of opportunities to watch how types work in the world of policing. From individual interactions to classes of recruits, type becomes evident if one watches for it. Type certainly isn't everything and personality is extremely complex, but students of type see the effects in everyday life. An example of recognizing type differences in groups occurred with a group of police officer recruits.

The Police Academy Setting:

Over several years, we administered the Law Enforcement Personality Profile® to 450 recruits in a large Southwestern police academy as well as the MBTI® to some. The LEPP was used to help recruits understand the police culture and the communication styles of most law enforcement officers. The policing culture was contrasted with the general public to help recruits understand differences in cultural communication and how other cultures communicate differently than police officers. Most questions and discussions focused on critical analysis of the subject matter. Approximately forty recruits were in each class; groups were together for ten to fourteen weeks before we spent several days with them, thus they knew each other well.

As with other studies, the results reflected general type distribution characteristics found in the previous 20 years of cognitive styles research. The majority of recruits (78%) preferred ST and NT cognitive styles. There were six or seven NFs and SFs in each class. As recruits were learning communication skills and cultural awareness issues, their comments and learning styles revealed typical characteristics of type. In discussing types after receiving the test results, we asked NFs and SFs if they felt different from the rest of the recruits in their class or from the general academy population at the academy. All stated they felt somewhat different from most of the instructors and other recruits.

Some NF/SFs wondered if the profession was for them or if they had mis-selected their career choice. Many recognized their preferences in communication and how they "looked at the world" differed from the majority of their classmates. When asked how they were different:

Male SF   *"I think I am more people-oriented, more compassionate, than most others in this class."*

Male NF   *"I think I am more compassionate than the rest of these slugs". (Laughter erupted from the class.)*

Other Feeling types would nod in agreement.

During these open discussions, classmates recognized each other's types and agreed with the assessments of other recruits. The STs recognized that the Feeling types seemed to be friendlier, people-oriented, and personally interactive with others. Recruits also recognized that the Thinking types personified the general culture of policing, while the Feeling types had an advantage in dealing with the community because of their obvious skills in relating to people on a more personal basis. The personality characteristics were easily recognizable to the classes.

Using a formal assessment to identify people's preferences is unnecessary if one understands and carefully listens to an individual's communication patterns. An example of informal evaluations occurred with a member of a class of forty-three:

A male recruit sat in the top row of the classroom's gradu-ated risers. He asked intellectually provocative and probing questions, and critically assessed the information presented about communication, culture, and different value systems. Other than speaking seriously to the subject, he did not smile or socially interact with the rest of the class during the morning session. His interactions and conversations with other class members were direct, structured discussions with critical analysis of the facts of what was being presented.

The Law Enforcement Personality Profile® identified his preferences as an ST. Upon receiving the assessment results, he raised his hand, "I don't really believe the results of this test. Doc, I don't think I am an ST, I think I am an NF." The rest of his classmates looked back and up at him quizzically. He then said seriously, "I really think I am a warm, friendly, compassionate sort of a guy." With that comment, some of his classmates burst out laughing. His classmates didn't believe his pronouncement. His actions during the training period reflected a strong preference for ST functioning. He was surprised that he wasn't perceived (ST) in the same manner that he felt (NF). When asked if he had a significant other at home, he replied in the affirmative. We asked him to take the completed instru-ment home and ask his wife to choose which of the four personality types fit him the best. In class the next day he looked a bit down and said, "She said that I am an ST."

All recruit groups stated they gained new insights into how the majority of officers preferred to function in the world of law enforce-ment, and how differences affected communication with members of other diverse communities.

During class interactions, numerous SF and NF recruits thanked us for the insight provided through the Personality profile. Many believed they were in the wrong profession or that something was wrong with them. The type and preferences provided a new understanding of their own and their classmates' behavior. They more fully understood the profession and the police culture, and believed they would be able to function better on the street because of the information.

Surveys of What the Community Wants in Law Enforcement Officers:

Citizens in various United States law enforcement and public safety jurisdictions are surveyed to learn about their expectations for law enforcement officers. These surveys have been given in most states through the years and usually reflect the same result. The Peace Officers' Standards and Training Board in Arizona (AZPOST) conducted a survey of citizens from 56 Arizona communities. Individuals assumed that officers could make an arrest, shoot a gun straight, drive a patrol car, and enforce the law. Knowledge of these tasks was a given.

Requested to identify community needs, citizens were clear that officers needed to respond to the community. Their primary requests were:

1. **Responsiveness.** "I want the officers in my neighborhood to communicate with us…talk to us and wave when you pass by. Do not drive or walk by just as if we weren't there."
2. **Compassion.** The second most common desire was for police officers to show compassion. They wanted police to act as if they really cared about the job and their role in the community.

These two initial community requests were surprising as most police officers expected crime prevention measures. The responses reinforced how communities desired better communication skills from officers who served them.

Officers and recruits are often urged to watch successful street officers. Officers who do best when working with informants and sources often solve the most cases. They learned to look at the world from an SF or NF orientation. The importance of communication and cordial interaction with the public are skills both recruits and officers must recognize and appreciate.

A well-known Canadian police administrator travelled the United States providing seminars on the importance of and how to develop communication skills in the profession. He finished his two-day presentation and was dining with a local sheriff and other police executives prior to his return home. One of the officers asked him to identify the one most important piece of advice on the topic. The Canadian administrator commented, "The best advice I can give is act like you give a shit." Caring is one of the best attributes to have in law enforcement.

Recruiting and Communication:

The importance of understanding personality types is again reflected in the recruitment process. To demonstrate the value of personality types, consider how a large police agency handled their recruiting process. The commander of the recruiting bureau reviewed all of the files and made the final decision on recruits coming into the academy.

- A new commander rotated into the recruiting position and brought individuals with him who he had worked well with in past assignments. The ST commander recruited his second in command, who was also an ST.

- The two were closely involved in the recruiting, interviewing, and supervision of the recruiting process. They had the final decision on which successful candidates would be hired. They assisted in the oral board selection that interviewed and tested the recruits.

- During the two years that both individuals headed the recruit-ing function, the vast majority of recruits entering the academy were STs, as one would expect. However, STs were hired at an even higher rate that one would usually find in a general police population; 90% of the recruits at the academy during those two years were STs and NTs.

- Several years later, an SF commander rotated into that same recruiting Bureau. He brought with him another individual as second in command. Both were SFs.
- During this tenure there was a noticeable increase in SFs and NFs entering the academy. NFs and SFs comprised 25% of the recruits, rather than the previous 10%, and they made it through the interview process in greater numbers than before.
- Many veteran police officers felt that the recruits coming out of the academy during this time period were "soft and too people-oriented." The assumption was they would get hurt on the street.

The different hiring cycles, one with an ST preference and one with an SF preference, reflected how individuals communicated best with others who shared the same cognitive style. The obvious penchant for similarity demonstrated why instruments and knowledge of mental processing preferences were useful tools for recruitment and law enforcement operations.

Birds of a Feather Flock Together

Officers tend to gravitate to job functions that best validate and support their strengths. At larger police agencies, policing tasks are assigned to specific commands or groups of officers. A large agency may have many units such as:

Traffic Enforcement	Community Relations	S.W.A.T. hostage negotiators
Neighborhood Patrol	Motors (motorcycle officers)	Personnel and Administration
Narcotics	School Resource Officers	Sex Crimes
Patrol	Homicide	

D.A.R.E & Gang Resistance Education and Training Officers

Invariably, a specific cognitive style preference can be found in each working group. Assigned to community relations bureaus from a variety of departments around the United States, a group of 45 Gang Resistance Education and Training officers were administered the Law Enforcement Personality Profile®. The Feeling to Thinking ratio was three to one; three Feeling preferences to each one Thinking preference.

Even a group of recruits could easily guess the cognitive preference of most officers working in a specific task group. When recruits in training were asked for the typical cognitive function of a Community Relations Officer, the class guessed "Feeling". School Resource Officers, D.A.R.E., and Neighborhood Policing officers were also identified as Feeling types. Most officers in a formal community relations function were Feeling types. Unsurprisingly, recruits stated "T!" when Motorcycle Traffic Officers, S.W.A.T., and the Drug Enforcement Bureau were considered.

A young officer, who had been on the job in patrol for three years, served as an example of how officers self-selected the areas that complimented their strengths. The officer completed the Profile assessment during his academy training and knew his cognitive style (NF). During a department planning meeting, he commented to his academy instructor about his career to date. His experience as a patrol officer on the street was interesting and successful, but he recently transferred to the Community Relations Bureau. With a broad smile, he stated that he loved the assignment, had found a real home, and planned to stay there for his entire career.

Similar types may group together by policing function. A major law enforcement agency hosted a day-long course on hate crimes. Leaders and members of various minority populations and members of the Gay and Lesbian community were invited to discuss questions like:

- "How do hate crimes affect your specific community?"
- "How can your community help the police in identifying and solving hate crimes?"

Approximately forty police department attendees were members of details assigned to assaults, homicide, property crimes, and officers from the Community Relations Bureau. Individuals from the investigative units were predominantly Thinking types, and those from community relations were predominantly Feeling types.

When the officers entered the room for the session, they sat together in their units; assaults with assaults, community relations with community relations, and homicide with homicide. The preference type and other group dynamics were observable based on the questions asked by the various groups of police officers and their reactions to the community panelists. The Feeling types discussed people issues and the Thinking types discussed statistics, figures, issues and concerns based on set criteria. Thinking types challenged presenters on the statistical and analytical information, while the Feeling types discussed issues from a personal point of view.

The pinnacle of the meeting occurred when the last member of the panel spoke. Having decided to not respond to the designated questions, the panelist spoke of a high-profile shooting incident that occurred the previous year. The suspect was shot and killed by officers after he confronted police with a shotgun. This panelist suggested police misconduct and liability was at issue and spoke of other emotionally charged topics (which had been legally resolved in favor of the police actions). The group of community relations officers listened to the panelist without interruption and quietly waited for him to express his concerns. The group of investigators asserted the panelist made factual misstatements and challenged the panelist's comments and stance. The room was emotionally charged, the meeting and presentations finished, and the speakers were thanked for their participation.

The meeting discussion was an exemplary instance of the differences in cognitive styles. Thinking types argued the factual errors. Feeling types considered the effect the shooting had on, and the challenge of building a dialogue with, communities. The interchange of ideas demonstrated differences in type and differences between the police culture and other cultures' communication context. The next and final chapter is focused on this dynamic.

CHAPTER 13

Police Personality and the Changing Cultural Community

Most law enforcement professionals tend to communicate differently than the majority of the public they serve. At least 80% of officers make decisions through Thinking, using logical, impersonal analysis. Studies involving communication styles show that Lower Context Cultures (like law enforcement) speak in ST terms, while Higher Context Cultures tend to speak in NT, SF, and NF expressions. As discussed throughout this book, the great majority of law enforcement officers prefer to take in information and process it through Sensing rather than Intuition, which means they are "bound in reality and pay attention to the here and now." Other personality measures with police populations from around the world seem to reflect the same results.

An opportunity to work with several groups of police officers from the Singapore State Police and the Singapore Airlines (S.A.T.S.) police occurred during a trip to the Far East and Singapore. The officers were all from Asian cultures, but still police officers performing tasks similar to police officers from around the world. Using the Law Enforcement Personality Profile® as a measure, one hundred officers reflected a three to one preference for ST and NT, the same ratio as officers in police departments in the United States. Several groups of Saudi Arabian police officers also reflected the same personality profile distribution as American and Canadian police officers.

For review, the general descriptors of law enforcement officers with ST or NT cognitive preferences were:

Concrete	Decisive	Traditional
Practical	Impersonal	Matter-of-fact
Observant	Structured	Precise
Logical	Factual	Pragmatic
Systematic	Detached	Direct

Individuals in the law enforcement profession spoke in direct, practical, and analytical terms and were seldom wrong about the facts. They were brief and businesslike. If forced to choose between tact and truthfulness, they chose truthfulness.

Police communicated in an ST manner the vast majority of the time. The ST/NT culture is reinforced through the media, particularly television with shows like Cops, Highway Patrol, The Canadian Mounties, and Dangerous Police Chases, which depicted action-oriented police work. Members of other cultures communicate more subjectively and personally.

Jungian type theory asserts that people are all individuals, but they share common ways of taking in information and making decisions. Cultural context is similar in that each person is related to, or comes from, a specific culture and shares, to one extent or another, characteristics of that culture. Cultural characteristics and how to behave in a culture are handed down through the generations.

Just like people, who have individual differences within the same personality type, so too are there individual differences within cultural contexts. People tend to behave as the majority of those from the same culture behave, but individuals also have personal habits and ways of being in the world. With that understanding in mind, the term "Context of Culture", and the cultural characteristics discovered by communication researchers, are reviewed.

Context of Culture

Recognized in the communication field for years but not extensively used, the context-of-culture approach facilitates an understanding of police culture and law enforcement's interaction with minority cultures. Context refers to the ways information is handled in communicating in a specific cultural group. Language carries a message, but various cultures interpret the meaning of the words and the way they are delivered differently. Communication context considers the relationship between the sender and the receiver, how language is used, and the body language involved (i.e., posturing, gesturing, and facial expressions).

Cultures can be placed along a continuum of lowest to highest. In the lowest context, words comprise most of the message. In the highest context, words, emotion, and emphasis combine and form the message. Cultures lower and another higher on the continuum do not reflect the idea that one culture is better than another. Anthropologist Edward T. Hall proposed the framework as a way to understand intercultural communication importance of understanding the context of a culture. People communicate with others through a range of abilities, including utilizing gestures, relationships, body language, and verbal or non-verbal messages. Although the continuum can be applied to organizations and cultural groups, "high-" and "low-" context culture typically refers to language groups, nationalities, or regional communities.

Lower Context Cultures

The cultures lower on the continuum are typically English, German, Swiss, Dutch, and Scandinavian. Law enforcement is a low context culture. To understand the message being communicated, direct verbal communication is necessary in low-context cultures. Individuals heavily rely on explicit verbal skills because individuals are not expected to have knowledge of each other's histories or background. Direct messages are necessary because individuals rely more on the spoken words than interpreting subtle or unspoken cues. Low-context communication is not shaped by long-standing relationships between speakers.

Verbal Communication

In low-context cultures, people are more concerned with the who, what, where, when, how, and why of issues rather than form. Direct and structured communication adheres to linear thinking and most of the message is conveyed through the structure of the words. As a language, English is a lower context lexicon. German, Dutch, and Scandinavian languages employ this direct communication style.

Verbal communication includes passing information between people, including values and the methods of exchange. Words send most of the message with specifics, details, facts, and explicit meanings relayed through the communication structure. Words and the process of communicating are more organized with less emotion conveyed during discussions.

In the TV show Dragnet, Jack Webb's "Just the facts, ma'am" is indicative of low-context communication:

- Minimal use of non-verbal elements. The message is carried more by words than with other non-verbal means.
- Verbal messages are explicit. Contexts in which verbal messages are spoken are much less important than the words.
- Exchange is direct. Information and ideas are spelled out exactly. Communication is seen as a way of exchanging information, ideas, and opinions.
- Disagreement is depersonalized. One withdraws from conflict with another and gets on with the task. The focus is on rational solutions, not personal ones. One can be explicit about another's bothersome behavior and comment on it.

Behavioral traits within lower-context cultures align with the general North American cultural values.

The majority of Americans draw their ancestry from lower context cultures. From the 2020 United States census, the top ten ancestry groups were:

1. German	6. American
2. Black/African	7. Italian
3. Mexican	8. Polish
4. Irish	9. French
5. English	10. Scottish

In the early days of America, the largest immigrant groups were from lower context cultures like Germany, northern Europe, and England. While the demographics may shift, the importance of culture remains a significant factor affecting communication in the United States.

Higher Context Cultures

Higher-context cultures include French, Italian, Arab and other Middle Eastern cultures. The highest context cultures are Asian, Hispanic/Latino, African/Black American, and Native American. High-context cultures are typified by harmony and group well-being preferences rather than individual achievement. High-context communication is usually relational and collectivist, with a focus on interpersonal relationships. A word's connotation (emotional or cultural association) is more important than the denotation (literal meaning). People within high-context cultures tend to be more aware and observant of facial expressions, body language, changes in tone, and other unspoken aspects of communication.

Verbal Communications

In higher context cultures, words send only part of the message and are much less important than the context of the message. The process of communication becomes more valued than the words used. Emotion, posturing, and gesturing may be part of the communication process. There is usually less direct eye contact, or deferred eye contact, and the exchange is more verbose and indirect. The process of communication may bury the explicit meaning of words within an implicit meaning, which is the true, intended message. The spoken message must be understood within the whole context of the conversation or discussion.

Higher-context cultures use and rely more on non-verbal elements, like voice tone, facial expression, gesture, and eye movement. The verbal message is implicit and context is more important than words. The person speaking prefers talking around a point, and may embellish to make an effective point, with most of the message's information carried in the physical acts and features of the conversation.

Communication is seen as a way to engage someone. Disagreement may be personal with people being more sensitive to conflict expressed in another's non-verbal cues. Conflict must be solved before work can continue, or the disagreement must be avoided because it becomes personally threatening. A good communicator is engaged in an art form.

Communication patterns in high-context cultures tend to be more complex than low-context communication. Asian, Hispanic/Latino, African/Black, and Native American cultures are all high-context communication cultures:

- Asians and American Indians use silence as a form of complex communication.
- Hispanic/Latino and African American cultures are more vocal and emotional, with less concern for direct meanings. This is true even if an individual from the culture has been in the U.S. for generations.
- Use of an expressive voice and language is highly valued among African/Blacks.

Typically, when law enforcement stops a car in Hispanic/Latino or African-American neighborhoods, people come out of their homes and gather around to see what is going on. They are interested in one thing - information - and may become expressive in their demands.

During a police officer training session on cultural awareness the discussion turned to stereotypes. The communication patterns of

Black American culture - more expressive and louder speech - were addressed by a Black officer:

"When my wife and I are having a rather strong discussion, there is a lot of volume and expressive force involved. The average White cop may think we are having an argument and are about to hurt one another. I want him or her to know that is not the case. We are just discussing. I don't want him to rush in and arrest one of us."

The conversational level may be louder in some neighborhoods and homes, with machismo behavior or emotion displayed. Higher context cultures often place significant value on the extended family and for individuals who are considered "family."

Matters of family and emotional, loud, or complex communication are in sharp contrast to policing. Although a high-context community may consider the culture or situational context as controlled, a lower-context culture or individuals with an ST or NT preference may not have the same perception. Law enforcement officers are typically trained to calm individuals, keep the peace, and restore order. Minority cultures will act to protect themselves and those related to them, and may feel powerless at times. Police represent power and, typically, young males challenge power - ergo they challenge law enforcement. A Black officer may receive more defiance than a White officer, especially in a Black neighborhood. In these interactions, race may be a pretext for the dynamics; power is the greater motive and race often used as an excuse.

A useful analogy, to help officers understand other cultures' value and concern for extended family, is when an officer is shot or hurt. Other law enforcement may not know the officer, but concern is expressed and different agencies band together in a demonstration of solidarity. Police organizations protect their "members", even if the officer is not formally affiliated with the specific department or agency. Individuals from cultures with an extended family structure feel the same concern. When a member of their culture or race gets into trouble, especially with the police, the entire "family" bonds together to protect the person and the community.

Immigrants:

Differences in culture and communication remain a concern for policing, particularly since law enforcement is relied on when immigration issues arise. Negative attitudes, regarding race and culture, may be held by individuals in the community, police, politicians, and other immigrants. In 1929, the researcher Charles Simon documented that many officers believed "that the immigrant population was composed of the mentally and morally unfit of Europe." Police had little or no tolerance for immigrants, even though many of the officers were recent immigrants themselves!

Law enforcement agencies pay attention to the nature and number of immigrants and refugees coming into their jurisdictions. Today, some Americans make statements like, "they take all our jobs" and "they impose their culture and don't even try to assimilate." Many newcomers are from high-context value systems, and are in direct contrast to the low-context value system which they enter. As emphasized in this book, the importance of understanding type as an important factor in communication styles. Understanding the interconnection, between cultural communication (high/low context values) and mental processing preferences, goes a long way in helping law enforcement officers better understand and do their jobs.

CHAPTER 14

Teaching in the Law Enforcement Profession

Educators and trainers all have their favorite teaching method(s). Cognitive preferences influence teaching styles, with success or lack of success often a result of failing to understand the audience's favorite cognitive processes. Many professors, consultants, and trainers have said they will "never try to teach a bunch of cops again." Instructors struggle with law enforcement audiences and rate students as too serious, critical, and cynical.

Police audiences are not very interactive or overly friendly, they do not want to play games, and are unwilling to participate in "fun" activities. Trainers seldom see the audience smile and may find them appearing somewhat uncooperative. Officers may struggle to enjoy themselves in learning situations, because the trainer's teaching style is different from their learning style. Consultants and educators who do not understand the differences cause misunderstandings. The group and the group's interaction suffers as a result of the trainer's ignorance.

Consider how an NF professor may approach teaching. The use of visual and performing arts may be employed - meditation, creative writing exercises, metaphors, symbolic representations or an activity using self-expressive strategies. Since details and specifics are neither high priority for Intuitive preferences, directions would likely be general, broad, and vague. The NF teacher enjoys presenting, because the techniques complement and reinforce their favorite way to learn. The NF teaching style may resonate with an NF learner, but the other learners may struggle. The power conveyed to the head of the classroom hinders the instruction, especially when a teacher fails to adapt to the students' needs.

An example of educational mismatch occurred at a large, Southwestern police department. Numerous groups, or cohorts, attended a Master's in Educational Leadership program at a state university. Cohort members ranged from officers recently out of the academy to assistant chiefs. The School of Education professors, many of whom were NFs, found the students challenging.

At the end of a course, a strong NF professor confided that she had not performed proficiently; with her education students, she usually felt she had done well. She was accustomed to students chatting with her after the final exam was completed. At the final class, most students socialized and told her how much they enjoyed the class. From the police cohort, half of the students got up, said "thank you" as they handed in the final exam, and left. She was concerned that she had not gained their confidence.

The mental preferences theory and the prevalent cognitive style of law enforcement (majority of officers were ST/NT) were suggested. As an ST- and NT- dominated profession, the students were likely approaching the final class in a logical manner, thinking about the next class in the program, and just moving on. While the behavior was perceived as uncordial, the students were not negative towards the instructor. In fact, when two students were asked why they left without speaking to the instructor, they both said they weren't even thinking about the class. They felt she was an excellent instructor and they were focused on preparing for the next class. Some students did comment about her organizational style:

- "she doesn't give specific instructions" or
- "she keeps changing the requirements on us" or

- "she isn't clear enough and just says to go ahead and anything we do on that subject matter will be fine."

This feedback would be expected from an NF-ST configuration. The typical ST requires structure and direction, even in an educational setting that adapts to learner needs. It may not be comfortable for ST students to just "go with the flow" when the directions are not as specific as they would like, or the subject matter is not presented in a manner that is as logical or structured as they would like.

Learning in ways that are different from our own cognitive styles can be difficult. A classroom assignment, using meditation music and instructions for everyone to close their eyes, will likely result in eye rolling and giggling from ST students. Asking them to take themselves "back in memory to a favorite childhood place where they felt safe and secure" and then draw a self-expressive, symbolic representation of that place could return loud guffaws from the audience. Explaining the differences in teaching styles, and how each style compliments mental processing preferences, provides a beneficial alternative to solely NF-focused activities. Teachers must be aware of and understand their own cognitive styles and those of their students.

Teaching Law Enforcement Officers from a Jungian Perspective

When presenting classroom materials to the cognitive styles within the law enforcement profession the following learning strategies, structure, and environment are helpful considerations:

- Assume the majority (80%) have a Thinking cognitive style (ST or NT). They will generally be serious, filter information through a logical-critical lens, and learn best through material focused on facts and logic.
- STs and NTs like to look at objective criteria and want to know what is expected. The goals and objectives of the class

or training session should be stated at the beginning of class, directions need to be accurate, and instructions included regarding how to do things.

- STs and NTs focus on efficient reasoning, deductive (parts to whole) and inductive (whole to parts), and may argue issues to the point of splitting hairs. They focus on rationality and practicality, wanting to know the what, when, where, and why; the people part of the equation - "who" - is of last concern. The Thinking preferences enjoy comparing and contrasting issues.

- The best way to get the message across to an NT/ST audience is to tell them why the subject matter is important to them and their profession. They enjoy demonstrating their proficiency and look for specific direction and guidance. Typically, STs want directions to be very specific, concise, and correct. They pay attention to detail and will find mistakes in dates, times, places, etc. Assignments with specific directions are appreciated; tell them how many pages, single or double spaced, what size font, cover sheet or not, and expected presentation style. Writing exercises and tests with question formats that require identifying the correct answer (True/false, Multiple choice, Fill-in-the-blank) are appreciated by ST/NT audiences.

- Case studies and discussion are preferred methods for presenting information. Structure learning as debates, lectures, and panel or group discussions, especially with topics and current issues that affect them. Focus the objective on finding alternative resolutions to events or provide opportunities for them to demonstrate specific skills or give reports/presentations to the class.

- ST/NTs are not usually found socially interacting with each other, but enjoy opportunities to speak to leadership about issues involving supervision.

Adapting to the majority's cognitive style (Thinking) does not mean ignoring the rest of the audience (SFs and NFs). Thankfully, the

Feeling types typically move right along with the STs and NTs, and naturally bring in the people-issues or subjective data for discussion.

The next case study outlines a successful methodology used to teach one of the toughest subjects in the profession - cultural awareness - to a law enforcement audience.

Teaching Cultural Awareness and Racial Sensitivity from a Jungian Perspective

The importance of cognitive style in teaching is critical to the success of cultural awareness training programs. The recommended methodology includes structuring the audience composition so that community members are not included when students are learning general facts and themes. There is a time and a place for bringing the two groups together, but not in the initial phases of the training.

Traditionally, training materials, including development, training, and consulting activities, were aligned to NF or SF cognitive preferences. Since the valuing viewpoint drives Feeling types, the methodologies stressed understanding diversity. Analogies were used to depict cultural differences (e.g., layers in a cake, slices of a pie, a rainbow's varied colors, etc.) Many curriculums were developed for private corporations and the objectives did not work well with law enforcement audiences. The cognitive styles of both the sender and of the receiver were ignored, including the power dynamics inherent in the law enforcement occupation. Any training for the policing profession must consider the power police have over citizens, in both their daily duties and their value systems. Programs designed to favor a specific process or cognitive preference will have minimal success or implementation longevity.

For even the most difficult subject matter, the following methodologies have demonstrated success with law enforcement:

- Information must be factual, realistic, concrete, and practical. From the outset of training, an instructor establishes the importance of a "no nonsense" rationale. Officers need to know pragmatically, logically, and objectively why it's important for them to spend time learning about these issues. Understanding the importance of becoming culturally competent needs to have a rational basis (e.g., makes their jobs safer, they gain community respect.)

- Individuals who make decisions using a Thinking cognitive style rely on analytical logic. This doesn't mean that officers do not have or share qualities of tenderness, compassion, or empathy; they just don't usually show them. With law enforcement professionals, the request to learn or to consider information needs to be directed to the head, not the heart. They are not persuaded by appeals to:

  ○ Issues of compassion, empathy, and congeniality;

  ○ A rationale of valuing diversity for the sake of social value; or

  ○ Valuing humanity over truth, justice, ethics, and fairness.

- Optimal classroom seating arrangement is five or six tables that seat four to five students at each table. Let students sit where and with whom they wish. Those of the same experiences, age groups, and values will usually sit together. Make sure the tables are set up so attendees are in groups of four, five, or six.

  ○ Less than four: students decide not to participate.

  ○ More than six: students splinter into smaller groups or decide to not participate.

- The classroom arrangement is an important consideration. If students are in a classroom or auditorium with the seats facing forward, the instructor is deemed "The Expert." In this physical arrangement, students employ seating choices to manipulate their participation. They find a seat where they can "sit it out" or a location best suited for "tripping up" an instructor, the latter choice being the more entertaining option. The rationale, for placing attendees in teams of four, five, or six, allows the facilitator to ask the group to consider questions or issues that are complex.

- The instructor's role is that of a facilitator, rather than a teacher. As often as possible, call upon various tables and individuals for comments and opinions. Doing so keeps attention focused on the subject and stimulates thought. Offering attendees an opportunity to express themselves shows respect, an acknowledgement of students' own knowledge and experience. The use of case studies and role plays also provides opportunities for officers to contribute their point of view.

- In planning activities, trainers need to be acutely aware of what each exercise is designed to accomplish. They must be willing to adjust the learning environment to ensure the objectives are met. Each activity should be structured to build on the preceding ones.

- Using a lecture method for instruction does not optimize learning. A trainer must trust the group's intellectual level and place attendees in teams for discussions. Individuals who may immediately react to an emotional or value-laden issue will be balanced by those who give the issues considerable thought and tend to speak later. Even the toughest group of police officers will contribute if allowed an opportunity. Attendees may not state it directly, but participants are listening; officers may modify their own biases and thoughts from what they hear and not "share" their learning with the group.

- Attendees should be engaged in active dialogue and exercises during most of the training sessions. Discussions with each other, performing pencil/paper exercises, and interaction with the instructor are key activities. The small group setting gives them the opportunity to continually interact with each other. Much of the learning in courses of this type takes place through the interaction between students. No matter what someone says about an issue or how pragmatically they may disagree, they will hear and consider other points of view from their peers.

- Avoid using numerical grading systems or specific critiques. Don't put too much stock in percentages or numbers as a measure of success. If administration insists on numerical rating as a performance measure of the instructor, put them in perspective. A presenter's facilitation skills should be rated separately from an instructor's knowledge of the material or subject matter. Allow some venting against the material - not the instructor. As a general rule, ratings are not as high in cultural awareness and racial sensitivity courses. This is due to the:

  o perception of the topic. Cultural awareness has been referred to as emotion negative training.
  o beliefs under examination. Individuals may have strongly held beliefs, which have likely been reinforced from on-the-job experiences. More often than not, on-the- street encounters are often negative everyday, so addressing officers' "reality" in relation to course content is imperative.

- Don't be concerned if the course outline or schedule is not followed "to the tee." Discussions are critical to learning and may become lengthy or involved. Some venting may be appropriate, but if the participants wander too far off, bring them back on course. Make sure the discussions are relevant to the topic.
- Sometimes planned activities "flop." Failure is rarely the result of teaching style; the composition of the group and their willingness (or lack thereof) to discuss the issues is more often the reason. If an exercise garners little reaction, then move onto the next activity without much comment. Some exercises work well with some groups, but may not affect others in quite the same way. Forge ahead! At least they are thinking, which is the objective.

- Even though individual cohorts may come from the same department, one group may be receptive and the next can be difficult. A trainer may feel "beat up" at the end of one session, while other groups of officers seem to click at the end of their sessions. This is generally the rule and not the exception.

- Trainers need to be committed to the issues being taught. They must be willing to dedicate time to personally expand their knowledge in these complex areas. Studying human behavior, keeping current on new research, and studying trends are paramount to success.

- Lastly, we highly recommend placing emphasis on the experience, ability, and intellect of the officers themselves. There is a vast amount of untapped knowledge within the law enforcement community in both sworn and civilian employees.

  - Let students discuss community concerns and the police response to these issues.

  - Give officers an opportunity to express themselves and become a part of the resolution process.

  - Allow officers opportunities to discover alternatives. Enable ownership of the solutions. Officers are the ones who have the most to gain (and probably the most to lose), so their mental, emotional, and physical investments are imperative for success.

Facilitation Skills

Two key points pertain specifically to a trainer's skills, which are critical for teaching cultural awareness and thus are spotlighted. A facilitator must be aware of and check their tendency for:

1. Knowing all the answers

There are few absolutes when addressing people's attitudes. Teaching classes about prejudice, racial discrimination, and gender issues can be "hot topics" and may trigger emotional - rather than logical - responses. Rather than trying to push a specific point of view, which often leads to resistance and resentment, keep in mind:

- The real goal is to stimulate thought and understanding. We just want to cause people to think, to re-examine their stereotypes and the way they have been socialized, and help them understand why they think the way they do about these issues. That, in and of itself, is enough to begin change and understanding.

- There will be situations of intense discussions that necessitate a trainers' intervention. Acknowledge that there may not be one, grand solution. Statements like, "I can't answer that", "I really don't know," or push back on the group and ask them "What do you think about that?" are authentic responses. Trainers often struggle with admitting their limitations, after-all, they are conditioned to know the answers to their subject matter. Trust in the intellectual acumen of the group. There are a lot of bright and experienced folks in the class who can contribute to making the class and content successful.

2. Being judgmental

All cultures are valuable; do not elevate one culture over another. Cultures are ethnocentric and all have been exploitive, sexist, racist, and colonialist during their existence. If a trainer is perceived as having a bias, the audience will react negatively. Tactics can be employed to promote non-judgmental perspectives, including situational interventions:

- People complain about being alienated during a session. Acknowledge their estrangement. Ask others in the room if they are feeling the same way. Allow for a dialogue to occur.
- Planned activities are not "clicking" with a group. Ask participants what they disagree with or aren't enjoying. Be prepared

to listen to their answers, as their responses will bring insight into their thought process.

- Disgruntled participation. An officer may say something like, "You have been off the street too long and don't know what is going on" or "You have never worked the street. How do you know what is going on out there?" If true, acknowledge the deficiency. Ask the audience for their perceptions about how "working the street" has changed. Trainers who acknowledge their student's perspective show they are listening to and are respectful of the officer's experience. However, personal exposure to situations doesn't alter the fact that individuals need to learn to deal with differences. Redirect the conversation by encouraging others to discuss the subject. A trainer who becomes defensive will lose balance in the classroom and create animosity with the audience.

Acknowledging comments or responses is often sufficient; an instructor may not have to say anything else. Most of the learning occurs after the attendee has left the session and has been thinking about the issues for a while. Changes are developmental and subtle. Mental thoughts take time to manifest into changed behaviors, especially for topics that deal with cultural awareness. Teaching about cultural differences is important because communities are constantly changing and officers must be prepared to understand and engage with fluctuations.

Process Versus Content: The Importance of Dialogue

Whether perceived or real, when issues of racial discrimination arise law enforcement is charged with understanding where a community is "coming from." Issues of prejudice, bias, gender and racial discrimination are inevitably emotional. Individuals are rarely restrained in their

They who only know one side of the case know little of that.
~ J. Stuart Mill

responses. When rage and violence are involved, invoking logic often results in offended sensibilities.

Compared to law enforcement, the general population is composed of individuals who make decisions using social value (Feeling) rather than impersonal logic (Thinking). When coupled with highly charged emotional issues, logical communication becomes difficult for Feeling preferences. Law enforcement professionals deal with advocate groups and minority communities whose representatives often make powerful assertions based on social value, which are not necessarily factual. Commissions and investigative committees are keen to say, "the time for waiting is over" or "the need for action is long overdue." Comments addressing suffering and injustices are commonplace.

Emotional appeals cultivate and trigger a hardwired, biological phenomenon in human anatomy. Without going into too much detail, basic structures of the brain carry out the same functions today that they did for our ancestors. Emotionally-charged experiences, like negative thoughts or rage, suppress the frontal lobe of the brain which is responsible for thinking, planning, memory, and judgment. People who feel aggrieved need to be able to express themselves; their sympathetic nervous system is on fire! When emotions are evidenced, individuals do not biologically have the capacity for constructive discourse. The parasympathetic system, which is responsible for calming the body, must be active for the frontal cortex functions to work.

Understanding human biology is important both in and out of the classroom.

- Communities need to be heard. Many members feel real rage for injustices done in their community. Dialogue must be allowed to happen. No matter how illogical, emotional, or off-base they may sound to police, comments need to be heard. The demands may seem inappropriate or impossible to meet, but they must be listened to and taken seriously. If opinions are denied or prevented, they will fester and serve as a barrier to real discussions. People's identities and sense of self are often tied to their concerns. Given a place at a forum and the respect to express themselves, people tend to transition from an emotionally-laden perspective to more problem-solving dialogues. Expect no real movement toward solutions if one fails to provide a space and time for them or if their comments are disrespected.

- Students need to be heard. When dealing with emotional issues in classes, participants may bring up contrary views, stereotypes, caustic anecdotes, and other hostile comments. Abuse may be heaped on the instructor and on the issue or community being discussed. An individual's personal ideas and, sometimes, self-esteem are under attack. A positive dialogue with a solution-based focus cannot occur - it is biologically impossible. As people say what they feel needs to be said, they then become aware of their own miss-statements and over-simplifications. Once expressed, the negative emotions become more moderate. This is called catharsis.

Once the tension is released through their own commentary, a person can often see a different perspective and begins to gain self-insight.

Gordon Allport, in his classic book *The Nature of Prejudice*, suggested that catharsis alone was not curative. The release of negative emotion provides an opportunity for the other side of the issue to be heard. If the original statements regarding race, culture, or stereotyping were exaggerated, slanted, or unfair (as they usually are), saying them aloud reveals the skew. It's like a mirror, reflecting back how one-sided their position is. When faced with information about themselves, people may seek a more balanced point of view.

One must be prepared for the emotion that will occur during these types of discussions. Hearing an emotion-driven, biased, one-sided characterization may incite emotions in others. People who hear the exaggerations may be struggling with their own personal prejudices. However, there will be individuals who can be called upon to modify the comments to be more balanced. Tap into this excellent resource by asking:

- "How about a comment about this from other members of the class?" or
- "What do the rest of you think?" or
- "What are you hearing in this discussion?"

The question interrupts the emotional spiral and also gives individuals more time to reflect on a reply.

Members of the police profession are problem solvers. Individuals in law enforcement may find listening for an extended period of time frustrating, because there is no focus on finding solutions to the problem. The rage and emotional language expressed by citizens with an SF or NF cognitive style of communication coupled with higher context cultures are the antithesis of how police approach "fixing" problems. More training or more programs are often proposed without allowing more dialogue to take place. By providing time and space for forums, encouraging members of the community to speak, and showing respect by listening carefully, people become more willing to engage in problem-solving dialogue.

Understanding cognitive styles and cultural contexts of communities are useful tools for communication and problem solving. Having different personality types in law enforcement, and the strengths of our associates, benefits our organizations. Using this knowledge to our best advantage moves policing towards facing the challenges, instead of relying on "tried and true" programming. Taking advantage of all the available tools will prepare the profession for 21st century challenges, which are sure to test us all. The quality of decision making is increased by merely including associates in the decision-making process. All you need to do is ask them to join.

CHAPTER 15

Benefits of Understanding Personality Differences

Understanding Jungian personality theory, by using the Law Enforcement Personality Profile™ and other Jungian Theory based cognitive instruments, is an excellent way to explain workplace behaviors. Jungian typology in the police profession can be used to:

- **Look at issues from different perspectives**. We can contrast the communication patterns in policing and arrive at an understanding of colleagues' viewpoints, including professionals that interact with law enforcement (e.g., social workers, reporters).

- **Aid in team building**. Those who understand various personality preferences are able to recognize and accept differences in communication styles, which contributes to a congenial, instead of antagonistic, work environment. As an example, an ST may bring necessary structure and reality to a group of N's who are intuitively dealing with an issue, while an NF may bring a global and compassionate perspective to a cold, stark, logical operation being planned by a group of STs.

- **Explain why individuals may feel uncomfortable in certain job situations**. The knowledge provided through theory and instruments helps us understand why some people excel in tasks and not others.

- **Assist with recruitment.** Applicants can understand the general culture of the work environment, the typical traits in the profession, and their personal strengths and weaknesses.

> **NOTE! The Law Enforcement Personality profile™ is *not* designed to be a predictor of behavior. It should *not* be used to screen out applicants. There are successful individuals, of every type, in all occupations.**

- **Support authentic communication.** We become more culturally aware when we consider communication patterns of others in different races and cultures. Additionally, understanding the communication patterns of other officers facilitates genuine listening and develops genuine dialogue. If we are not constantly trying to decipher "why" someone expresses themselves the way they do, we can devote our energies to "what" they are stating.

Policing, like other occupations, has a vernacular that helps officers understand situations. By referencing and comprehending mental processing preferences, officers are equipped with a language for understanding people and their communication patterns.

Psychological surveys, like the Law Enforcement Personality Profile ®, should not be used to predict an individual's ability to perform a specific job. Persons of all cognitive styles can perform the job of policing. Although the majority of the people in law enforcement have a cognitive style preference for Sensing-Thinking, one cannot assume all STs make good police officers. Certainly Intuitive-Feeling types, who comprise only 6% of the officers in the profession, add to the quality of law enforcement (even if their strengths do not necessarily speak to the general tasks of the job.) If the results from the Law Enforcement Personality Profile ™ were used to screen out individuals who didn't fit the ST profile or to recommend applicants not seek a job in the policing profession, the diversity that uncommon types bring to the occupation is lost. Consider the research results reflected in this book; roles in law enforcement require different approaches and the demand for community policing is only increasing. More, not less diversity, is necessary as the role of law enforcement adapts to new social arrangements.

For team building, Jungian typology and the various personality types facilitated problem resolutions for a work environment that was constantly changing. For example, the following scenario demonstrated the pitfalls of a likeness and the potential of typologies:

- The chief of a major police agency was an Intuitive-Thinker. He had two assistants, an NT and an ST. The chief communicated well with both assistants, but spoke more of change and general conceptual operational issues, such as reorganization, with the NT.

- Both NT administrators travelled to various conferences and symposiums together, because both communicated well together in global terms. They would discuss new technology and attempt to institute change within the organization, albeit unsuccessfully.

- The issue of change was discussed during a team building session using Jungian Cognitive Styles. It became evident that the persons who favored the NT preference were too global in their applications and with the re-organizational issues. The NTs were missing numerous details necessary for the successful implementation of any change.

- Because of their familiar communication patterns and ease of understanding between each other, the NTs inadvertently excluded the ST administrator from the critical areas of discussion – the actual details necessary to implement change.

- All three administrators agreed that the ST preference would serve as a "leavening agent" in the planning discussions. By strategically aligning personality strengths with job tasks, they ensured a methodical, step-by-step process was used to implement department changes.

Having been trained in Jungian typologies, the three administrators had the foundational knowledge to assess the situation and determine a course of action. They developed a plan - together - which facilitated an improved tactical approach to the challenge. This occurred because they 1) had the knowledge of Jungian typologies, 2) knew the strengths and weaknesses of the profiles, 3) communicated effectively using the Jungian verbiage (had the language to understand each other), and 4) trusted the information about typologies and each other.

The Law Enforcement Personality Profile® (LEPP) was used in the operational areas of a police organization dealing with communication styles. An NT deputy chief recognized that a more acceptable "tone" was needed when issuing written directives to the organization's sworn officers. The typical blunt writing style of NTs and STs negatively affected both groups. In an effort to communicate in a more conciliatory tone, the administrator asked an NF individual to review memoranda prior to distribution. Referred to as "one of his few token feelers", the NF made changes to the tone of the communication, not the content, to give the message a more "humane" touch.

Another example occurred with a group of police managers whose pragmatic approach occurred after a team building session. An ST individual chose members of a planning committee by selecting competent individuals from each of the various personality types. The objective was to collect input from as many points of view as possible. The manager wanted:

- Sensing-Thinking types, who brought facts and present realities into the discussion;
- Intuitive-Thinking types, whose global, planning perspective was a needed strength;
- Sensing-Feeling types, who focused on practical, caring solutions for the people involved; and
- Intuitive-Feeling types, whose innovative, insightful ideas for dealing with people issues was required.

The diversity of perspectives helped the committee efficiently and effectively reach the planning goals with minimal conflict.

Knowing how different personality types function provides an understanding as to why some officers perform better at some tasks than others. As an example, an investigator at a large, suburban detective bureau had risen through the ranks from a uniform patrol officer.

- He was never content or comfortable in the profession. While he was able to perform the job in a satisfactory manner, he always seemed to be at loose ends. He was not "really fitting in" with the rest of the officers.

- Other officers felt he was "kind of drifty." He did not stick to the task at hand and seemed to go in a lot of different directions.

- Through results of the Law Enforcement Personality Profile®, the investigator determined he had an Intuitive-Thinking preference, with his dominant being Intuition. After an explanation of these preferences, he began to understand why he was uncomfortable around Sensing types, why they didn't accept him, and why he didn't quite fit in.

- He transferred into a research-based job working with computers, intelligence data, and special projects. With the job shift, he became a strong contributor to the investigative process.

He enrolled in graduate school with the intention of becoming a counseling psychologist after retirement from policing.

A similar example occurred with a patrol officer in a large city. He was assigned to the road for several years and enjoyed being a cop, but was very uncomfortable with motorist confrontations and the unpleasant duties in traffic accidents. Even though he was talented in his ability to deal with people, he considered leaving the profession. His Personality Profile results showed a clear NF preference (the cognitive style of only five percent of police officers.) Understanding this, he sought and obtained a transfer into the photographic and media unit where he had outstanding performance reviews.

To review:

- Feeling types (NFs and SF) recognize their difference; they are not the typical personality type for policing. NT and ST are the predominant cognitive styles in law enforcement occupations and typify most police officers.

- Intuitive-Thinking (NT) types and Sensing-Thinking (ST) types make decisions using analytical, objective, logical criteria. STs and NTs seem to get along well with each other because they share the same Thinking method of making decisions (impersonal, analytical logic).

- NT and STs have a Perception difference. Perception is the taking in of information prior to making a decision, which is usually non-verbal. Sensing (S) and Intuition (N) are often "visible" through action. NTs are more global and future-oriented; STs are more grounded in detail than looking ahead or "down the road." STs are better at remembering details in the present.

An example of global thinking or thinking ahead (and not having "in the moment" details) occurred with an NT deputy chief. He knew he was different from other city commanders; when other captains reported to duty in the morning, they would go through the previous night's incident reports to see what went on in their district. When he was a captain, he assumed he would be told about the details if something occurred during the night shift. Reflecting on his career, he relayed the following story:

> "We were riding through the district and there was a call about a robbery of a convenience store that had just taken place. I was driving and my partner said, "Come on, we gotta go to this convenience store." I said to him, "We're not going to catch him by going up there. He's long gone from there." I said, "Let's drive by the other convenience store in our district and maybe we'll get lucky"… We drove up a side street, turned the headlights off and drove down to the cross street, and as we got to the intersection, the guy came running out with a shotgun… We bailed out of the car and chased him and caught him. It turned out there was a car up the street a ways where

there was another guy, the lookout, with a driver. It seemed they had done three other very vicious stick-ups. If Bob had been driving we would have gone to the convenience store that was robbed because that's what you do".

As an NT, he was not good with remembering names, license plates, or detail. He never found a stolen car and commented that the only way he would know a car was stolen was "if it ran into me on the street."

Attention to detail, or not being good at detail, is often the difference between STs and NTs. Yet, NTs and STs don't usually see the difference because taking in information (using the Perceiving function of S or N) is not an outwardly, visible process. The Judgment functions of Thinking or Feeling are observable. Upon reaching a decision, a Thinking type can relay the pros and cons of their decision with a critical analysis of the facts. The Feeling type describes the impact on people and stresses the human values that contributed to their decision. STs and NTs share the same Judgment function, but may not easily recognize their S/N differences.

The benefits of knowing how and why we best function was captured in the example of an ST/NT team who were part of a crime scene search group. The NT performed the crime scene search, including finding evidence, mapping locations, bagging up evidence, and other detail work. Invariably, the ST found additional evidence missed by the NT. The reason: the NT's preferred method of Perception caused him to skim over the scene and miss important details.

Another example of team member incongruence occurred when an NT officer was asked to design an occupational physical testing course for recruits and veteran officers.

- The course was a substitute for the typical physical standards measurements test, the standards of which had come under scrutiny for being unrelated to the job.
- On a large whiteboard, the NT designed a complex, comprehensive course, drafted the specifications, and began to seek out the materials and labor to complete the job. His ST supervisor asked for a comprehensive written document

detailing exactly what he was doing and how he intended to accomplish the job. The ST was just asking for a detailed explanation and covering all of the bases, as STs do.

- Upon hearing these demands, the NT seemed to lose the "wind out of his sails." To him, he had been moving forward and was past the need to write about the plan. He was busy getting the job done and "skipping steps," as NTs often do.

The NT had to stop and cover all of the bases before continuing.

Another example of cognitive differences occurred with a recruit who continually forgot small items like a specific uniform part needed for the day, or a tag, or PT equipment. He usually had a good memory for such things and was at a loss in trying to understand why he was forgetting the items. When questioned about his experiences prior to coming to the police academy, he indicated he was a part-time research assistant at the university he attended, enjoyed reading history books, and graduated with a political science degree. He enjoyed art, drama, and other intellectual pursuits, traits that were typical of individuals who preferred to take in and process information intuitively.

When he entered the highly structured life at the police academy, he struggled with the detail required to succeed. Additionally, the very issue of being in a somewhat stressful academy situation affected all the recruits' abilities to concentrate and pay attention to detail. After learning about cognitive differences, he kept a structured, daily list of what was needed for the following day. Although he felt the list was a "crutch," the inventory enabled him to successfully complete the academy. When he graduated, he was also knowledgeable of what the occupation required and what would be necessary for him to fit in and be successful in the profession.

As you can see through the examples in this book, the Sensing Thinking Types and Intuitive Thinking Types, the less common Sensing Feeling Types and the least common Intuitive Feeling types can all perform the tasks of policing. All of the various types bring differing strengths to the profession. The more we understand individuals and their various preferences for action, the closer we can come to a better understanding of the profession itself. Personality and behavior are extremely complicated. Viewing police behavior through the lens of Jungian personality types gives us an excellent opportunity to observe the complex world of police behavior in a completely different light.

Stephen M. Hennessy, Ed.D.

PART THREE

Understanding Police Through the Millenial Generation in Policing

CHAPTER 16

Generational
Theory and Policing

Generational cohort research has an abundant footprint on popular and academic literature. A generation is defined as a group of people who have similar life experiences concurrently developed due to historical events. These similar life experiences affect an individual's worldview both personally and professionally. Individual anomalies may exist within a generation, but this research focused on generational commonalities. Members of a generational cohort are generally bound together by historical world events that create a context for life, and this context appears to be carried and replicated through life. The private sector has more generational literature than the public sector, and policing has nearly none. Generational divides appear to exist in all American workplaces, yet policing is different because of its culture. Our research combined generational literature of private industries with many civilian public sectors to include military and correctional references similar to policing.

The five major generations currently in the American workforce are the (a) Traditionalists, born prior to 1946, (b) Baby Boomers, born 1946-1964, (c) Generation X, born 1965-1979, (d) Generation Y or Millennials, born 1980-1995, and (e) Gen Z, born after 1995. Researchers have assigned slightly different year demarcations for generational cohorts, but our dates are generally accepted. Each generation possesses and exhibits unique beliefs and values in the workplace developed from their shared life experiences through the history of the time. These unique beliefs and values may positively or negatively affect the workplace through lack of understanding or communication. It is clear the literature on generational differences is growing, but it is unclear if generational differences and characteristics are identifiable and generalizable across a single or multiple work industries. Each generation exhibits unique strengths and weaknesses in the American workforce. Generational diversity in the workplace is not a new subject, but it has become a highly investigated topic in contemporary peer-reviewed and popular media literature (yet, not in policing).

Organizational decision-makers would benefit by identifying genuine generational differences through research data rather than relying on popular media literature. Distinctive expectations and motivators exist amongst each of the diverse generations: (a) Traditionalists, (b) Baby Boomers, (c) Generation X, and (d) Millennials. At the time of this publication, Gen Z were beginning to enter the workforce, so not much research has been compiled to date. A legitimate research study might assist in identifying generational characteristics that organizational leaders could utilize for hiring, satisfaction, and retention.

Members of each generation are subjected to and influenced by cultural, societal, and family events that occurred during their formative years. The formative years are generally accepted across the literature as pre-teen through teenage years of life. As individuals develop through their formative years, various historical events impact each generation differently and are openly displayed or remain latent for a lifetime. These historical events are what usually bind an individual to a particular generational cohort. Again, anomalies may exist due to life events that differ from the general generational population.

Individuals born somewhere near the widely-debated birth-year demarcations or within a few years of the generational split are known as "Cuspers". Cuspers sometimes have the ability to move between two different generational cohorts due to the historical events that bind Cuspers during their formative years. For example, generational Cuspers may not fall in line with the norms and characteristics of a single generation. However, Cuspers usually identify with the generation that most closely fits their underlying values and lifestyle characteristics identified throughout their lifetime.

Traditionalist Generation (Born prior to 1946)

Members of the Traditionalist Generation are usually defined by the Great Depression. These individuals grew up in an era of great economic hardships and self-sacrifice. Their core values were usually a life sacrificed to an employer and conformity to the general society. Traditionalists are described as patient, loyal and they put work before play.

Traditionalists represent over 59 million of the present-day employees in the workplace. They want to continue to make a difference in their organizations through challenging and stimulating work. Professional growth and learning for Traditionalists come through hands-on experiences, and they appear to have difficulty with the fast-paced changes in technology. We found that Traditionalists actually have a positive view of technology, but they may require more training due to their unfamiliarity with the new and often changing technologies.

Members of the Traditionalist generational cohort appear to work well with patient Millennial mentors. Millennials appear to focus on their relationships with the older generation as they explore technologies, such as social networking with them. Matching Millennials with Traditionalists in law enforcement may have an immediate positive organizational impact.

Traditionalist employees often exude extreme loyalty, self-discipline, and organizational knowledge to their superiors. Many in this generational cohort have retired from the workplace, but continue to value a working lifestyle through volunteering or part-time employment. The apparent diversity of blending Traditionalists with Millennial employees in the workplace could cause collaboration and conflict which requires further research beyond the scope of this book.

Baby Boomer Generation (1946-1964)

In contrast to the Traditionalist Generation, individuals from the Baby Boomer Generation generally grew up with drastically changing economic and political events. For example, during the formative years for a Baby Boomer they likely experienced the Vietnam War, Martin Luther King, Jr. and John F. Kennedy assassinations, as well as Watergate, increased feminist ideologies, and Woodstock. Baby Boomer family units also moved from urban to suburban areas into homes, and for the first-time families owned multiple cars. Raised by strong work-ethic parents, the almost 80 million Baby Boomers entered the workforce at a furious pace like never before in American history. To get ahead in the workforce, this competitive, hard-working generation started to work more than the standard 40 hours per week. There are varying opinions about the positive or negative impacts of the increased work hours introduced and maintained by members of the Baby Boomer generational cohort.

Today, over 76 million Baby Boomers still occupy the American workplace, and they are often found in positions of higher authority in organizations due to workplace experience and seniority. They often define work ethic as long hours and in-person work. This Baby Boomer approach to vocation and their definition of work ethic are displayed in both management and followership styles. Therefore, Baby Boomers are less likely to push against their superiors while spending long hours at work and away from their families.

Baby Boomers have created an organizational cultural value in the number of hours a person spends working as well as the amount of money paid for working. This face-time, butt-in-seat, at the workplace, organizational institutionalization is respected and desired by Baby Boomers, but not Millennials. Many Baby Boomer organizational leaders complain about Millennials who do not fit the company mold, yet they themselves created them as their own children. This workplace leadership incongruence can often conflict with the workplace behavior and acceptance of the younger Millennial Generation employees.

Generation X (1965-1979)

The work-driven, many-hours working environment implemented by Traditionalists and Baby Boomers developed the unique members of Generation X through a pseudo-rebellion against the long work hours away from the family. As a result, Gen X members became independent and adaptable employees who saw their parents' loyalty to employers rewarded with layoffs and considerable cutbacks. The increase of divorce and mothers going to work resulted in latchkey kids who helped raise their siblings autonomously. These negative formative years' experiences translated into the current informal, self-reliant Generation X employees and bosses.

The constant need for independence in the workplace, and the dislike of micromanagement comes as a result of their lonely albeit autonomous upbringing. Gen Xers prefer to receive and give feed-back immediately in an informal manner. Work must be fun, loosely structured and combined with many opportunities for personal and professional growth. Career options are usually viewed as open to Generation Xers who watched their parents' reduction in force and layoff in the 1980s. They may prepare for their opportunistic departure from an employer due to an economic downturn as a defense to their parents' negative experiences during the Generation X formative years. A Generation Xer will often have an eye on a few new job opportunities or even an entirely new industry ready to go at a moment's notice.

Members of Generation X take their employment status seriously, but they are continuously building their personal resumes in preparation for lateral or external opportunities. This behavior may be a result of trying to obtain employment that allows the Generation Xer to maximize time spent with their families. In cross sectional data from the Families and Work Institute, 52% of Generation X was family centric as compared to the 40% of Baby Boomers. This may suggest some of the current conflict between work, life, and family balance that Generation X experiences in the workplace with their Baby Boomers supervisors. These Generation X workplace satisfiers may also be in conflict with the Millennials and is further discussed in this section on police personality

Millennial Generation (1980-1995)

Research literature commonly identifies the latest generation in the workplace to be the most diverse. More specifically, Millennials are identified by their unique dress, body piercings, tattoos and constant electronic connectivity rather than just race and gender. As a generation who was constantly showered with attention and praise, Millennials are often described from confident to arrogant. The Millennial Generation has been referred to as self-absorbed trophy kids who aspire to be financially successful, with strong global/environmental and socially-responsible consciousness.

Millennials are uniquely different because their individual goals and desires seem to conflict yet they, interestingly, work well together. For instance, contemporary popular and research literature often depict Millennials as narcissistic and egocentric, yet they are also described as the most philanthropic generation in history as reported by the Pew Research Center in 2010. Maybe these contrasting behaviors and beliefs are why Millennials are described as confident, assertive, entitled, yet more miserable than ever before.

Differences in behavior internal to the Millennial Generation is also described. Millennials desire strong supervision and direction in the workplace, but demand the flexibility to complete tasks on their own terms. Some Baby Boomers and Generation Xers refer to the Millennial Generation as the most difficult generation to work with, but further qualitative research is required to identify the root cause of this legitimate or perceived revelation.

According to a 2010 Pew Research Center report, Millennials identify their generational uniqueness through (a) technology, (b) music/pop culture, (c) liberalism/tolerance, (d) intelligence, and (e) clothing. Values listed by the other three generations in the workplace included items such as (a) honesty, (b) work ethic, and (c) respect/morals. Without this deeper investigation and research directly from Millennials, it could be too easy to conclude their uniqueness would greatly contrast with the other generations in the workplace. Therefore, the generational discussion in this book focuses mainly on Millennial-age employees.

Generation Z (1996 to current)

Compared to other generations, only 40% of Gen Zers are non-Hispanic. A quarter of Gen Zers are Hispanic, 14% black, 6% Asian and 5% are two or more races or are of another race (Pew Research Center, 2020). Unlike Millennials, who came of age during an economic recession, Gen Z were set to enter the workforce with a strong economy and record-low unemployment. At time of this publication, COVID-19 reshaped the world of opportunities. The Pew Research Center reported half of the oldest Gen Zers (ages 18-23) stated that they or someone in their household had lost a job or taken a cut in pay because of the economic shutdown (Pew Research Center, March 2020). Gen Z workers were more vulnerable to job loss because many worked in the service industries. More than older generations, Gen Z looks to the government to solve problems, rather than businesses and individuals. As Gen Z continues to participate in the workforce more data will be useful for understanding the values and motivations of the generational cohort. Since Millennial's are in the current law enforcement pipeline, and few Gen Zers, much of our data and information remains focused around the other 3 main cohorts (Boomers, Gen X, and Millennials).

Millennials and Workplace Satisfaction

The cohort of individuals born since 1980 (Millennial Generation) are the current generation impacting the workforce, including America's law enforcement departments. Researching the most recent generation of employees affecting the workplace is not unique, but identifying the root causes of workplace satisfaction in policing through the Millennial voice is necessary for high customer service and retention.

We support the proposition that Millennial employees behave differently in the workplace, but most employers apparently fail to integrate the needs of successive generations. Before even being hired, traditional thinking in policing instructs new employees to adapt to the existing organizational technology and culture … or go away. This workplace model is supported by police-themed television and movie culture, which does not provide the best satisfactory work-place environment for high-speed Millennials. Increasing workplace satisfaction and retention comes from creating the best environment for Millennials who want to become law enforcement officers and use their natural talents.

Work attitudes of Millennial employees are consistently compared to the two previous generations, Baby Boomers and Generation X, in the workplace. It is incumbent upon the leaders of the two older generations to provide the necessary workplace environment for their youngest employees to succeed and thrive. As discussed earlier, Millennial employees viewed workplace responsibilities and compensation as lower factors for job satisfaction with personal and professional advancement potential and free time as other high-attention factors. This workplace attitude is clearly different from Baby Boomers and Generation X. Millennial employees are not satisfied with the common and rigid, rules-laden, command and control workplace currently in policing and legislated by the Baby Boomers and Generation X leaders.

Millennial Generation values, attitudes, and experiences are technologically proficient. Millennials are highly educated and constantly connected to social groups through the internet. When compared to Arizona Peace Officer Standards and Training Board's standards for educational requirements, the Millennial Generation generally exceeds the minimum qualifications of high school diploma or general equivalency diploma with some college. Government work may present too few workplace opportunities and promotions, which fails to fully engage Millennials. We believe Millennials may simply be bored with their current level of responsibility provided by their government jobs. Workplace challenges and genuinely solicited input are important to maintain Millennial employee engagement.

Millennials assert a much higher level of flexibility when communicating to bosses and expect to have a valid voice in the workplace. Millennials wish their voices to be heard by their bosses as well as their teammates, and this expectation factors into workplace satisfaction. Employers are willing to advertise, recruit, hire and train Millennial employees, yet appear unwilling to place them on committees or allow them organizational input. Therefore, the best talent is not always retained in organizations due to overly-stringent government workplace policies. Every Millennial-aged officer can be a leader in their organization to help propel workplace satisfaction of their peers, because they are not just the future of policing, they are "the now." The Millennial Generation may have to take the lead in making workplace changes to provide the most satisfying workplace environment rather than waiting for current managers to act. These implications were acknowledged in our research through identification of Millennial workplace satisfiers and motivators.

For job satisfaction, Millennials rank highest benefits, praise/ recognition, personal happiness, and flexibility for job; job security ranks at the bottom of the list. Due to the recent blending of the industrial and mechanized era with the computerized information age, choices of contemporary American industries are plentiful for Millennials. Law enforcement leaders must be aware of the motivators for Millennial-aged employees, as Millennials today have choices of employers as well as industries to provide the job satisfaction they seek. Police organizations are not just competing for Millennial-aged employees with other police agencies. Millennials are willing to look across multiple industries to identify the employer and industry that meets their workplace satisfaction needs. Millennials have no reservations about quitting a job that does not satisfy their list of needs and moving back home with their parents to search for another job. There appears to be no stigma associated with such a decision for the Millennial Generation.

Technology is one of the great satisfaction dividers between Millennials and other generational cohorts. About 75% of Millennials are connected to the internet every day, while only 40% Baby Boomers tune in as often (Taylor & Keeter, 2010). The constant use of mobile cellular technology can be a point of contention for Millennials and their older bosses. The overwhelming majority of Millennials (87%) prefer to communicate via text messaging (Cekada, 2012) and they often prefer to only communicate in this manner. This communication divergence can cause organizational conflict that leaders must better comprehend for organizational effectiveness. Technological communication in the workplace must be further researched to identify workplace behaviors and tools to improve communication and satisfaction.

The technological, external hygiene factors for Millennials in the workplace are plenty. Because Millennials were raised during the digital age, they have a unique and competitive edge with contemporary communication and computing. Technology often increases the speed of decisions and deliverables, and this quickened pace can often result in Millennial employees appearing to be impatient and unsatisfied to older generations. The advanced technological skill of Millennials sets them apart from previous generations in the workplace, but exists to support high job satisfaction. Proactive organizational leaders could blend technology ideas from Millennial employees in communication decision-making and budgets.

Millennials also prefer working in teams as a job-context hygiene factor. Millennial employees have most likely been placed in team atmospheres by their parents their entire lives to this point. Working together to problem-solve has been the main learning point of their schooling, sports and extracurricular activities. Therefore, Millennials tend to look down upon the individualistic cut-throat political and bureaucratic rigor of the previous generations. Millennials prefer workplace collaboration to the compromise of politics.

A more relaxed dress and workplace atmosphere are highly desired by Millennials through casual work days or more relaxed work uniforms. A quick look at the laidback workplace environments of Google, Red Bull, Facebook and Zappos are employers very well known to Millennials who offer extremely informal workplace environments. Para militaristic workplaces may have to reexamine their utilitarian dress code/ideologies to attract and maintain highly satisfied Millennial-aged police employees.

Some intrinsic workplace motivators for Millennials also exist. Millennials embrace social networking as they appear always plugged in and using the latest technology. They strive for self-improvement and advancement through employer-provided training, and they want to reach their career goals much faster than previous generations. This is often interpreted as impatience and entitlement by older generations of bosses and coworkers.

A work-life balance is also mandatory for Millennials. Work and the environment must be fun. They expect to work collaboratively with their bosses rather than just for their bosses, which can be a challenge for some older generation leaders. All of the extrinsic factors and intrinsic motivators for Millennial-aged employees are important for organizational leaders to know, because research indicates employees in their twenties can be expected to stay in one position for just 1.1 year! This high-level of turnover will negatively affect organizations through budgets and reduced customer service unless transformational leaders identify the issues and make the appropriate adjustments.

Police Culture may be incompatible with Millennial Satisfaction

It is not unusual for beliefs and values of succeeding generations to be incompatible in the workplace. Law enforcement agencies that espouse problem-solving community policing for their officers appear to be incongruent with their internal Para militaristic, bureaucratic organizational structure, which reduces officer morale. For example, asking officers to have high external kindness and customer service for those they serve while, internally, administration treats them bureaucratically and militaristically does not match the original message sent by law enforcement leaders.

The intense managerial environment in policing targets employee performance, establishes unclear work priorities, and engages in workplace practices that negatively affect officers. Entrepreneurial, individual initiative is not embraced in militaristic cultures such as police organizations. Forcing the youngest generation of employees to adapt to the organizational tools and systems currently in place (or get out of the organization) may not be the most effective police business model. Millennial-aged officers appear sensitive to this phenomenon, especially as it is incongruent with their worldview, beliefs, and values taught to them in the formative years.

Millennial-aged police officers are frustrating today's police supervisors, which in turn contributes to low Millennial police officer satisfaction. The past two decades has drastically changed what is expected from today's police officers as well as shifting police culture philosophies. Officers have been asked to shift from distant enforcers of the law to more friendly community-based police officers. Most law enforcement organizations failed to incorporate the desires and preconceptions of the Millennial Generation of police officer to these contemporary philosophies. For example, Millennial employees prefer flexibility, autonomy, and work-life balance from their employers, and they highly prefer a more informal work environment, yet the strict police culture of rules, regulations, and uniforms has negatively affected Millennial satisfaction. Police departments with flexible workplaces with opportunities for personal growth and freedom are the most satisfying organizations for Millennials. The specific workplace factors and personal growth motivators have yet to be identified for police organization dissemination and practical application.

Generational conflicts in policing are traced to differences in culture, values, and communication styles obtained during the formative years. Older generation police officers, generally Baby Boomers, are staying longer in workplace, therefore maintaining the cultural status quo. This long-term workplace culture is in opposition to the short-term, immediate ideology of Millennial-aged employees. Police recruiters discuss 20 to 30-year careers and retirements with an entire generation of prospective Millennial employees who are very poor at long-term planning, and may actually prefer to have multiple employers or careers. This generational conflict increases in strength due to a misinterpretation of Millennials' desire for multiple employers as a lack of organizational loyalty. Perhaps, it is simply a different view of employment that can be properly addressed by informed police leadership.

As community policing gained popularity over the past few decades, current research indicates agencies continue to train police recruits within militaristic and bureaucratic cultures. Millennials crave the structure but require higher levels of praise than previous generations, which frustrate older supervisors and coworkers. This is Millennial behavior that is often misinterpreted by police instructors as Millennial entitlement. Millennials also reported being part of a group and personal achievement as high factors for satisfaction, yet policing teaches an autonomous style of service delivery. Police officers are trained to work alone in patrol cars to answer calls for service. The real team effort only comes during training days together or on large crime scenes or calls for service. The strong desire to work as a team is an internal satisfier, yet riding around in a patrol car all shift alone may be a dissatisfier.

Leaders may also discover independent thought is lacking among the Millennial Generation due to overprotective parenting. A common term in the research literature as well as popular media for Millennial parenting is helicopter parent. This type of parent hovers over their children protectively making daily decisions and diminishing personal growth. Proactive police organizations must be prepared for the new workplace challenges for Millennial-aged police officers for greater customer service and employee satisfaction.

The usual government politics in policing are unappealing to this youngest generation. To obtain or maintain Millennial employee satisfaction, teamwork should be the focus of police managers rather than competition. Politics must be trained as a form of social net-working to Millennial officers, rather than the usual barrage of political negativity experienced through the news or from parents. Working and performing in these types of social groups and teams is natural for the Millennial, so enhancing their satisfaction should improve customer service. Their accepted police structure appears to be teamwork-oriented; changing leadership to a participative management style in which Millennials are heard and respected is necessary for high police officer satisfaction.

The current bureaucratic organizational culture of policing is working against the retention of Millennial employees. The archaic philosophy of throwing employees into a job and letting them sink or swim simply does not make sense to Millennials. We recommend employers/leaders create flexible environments for Millennial employees to flourish, contribute, and utilize natural talents and education. Policing policies, rules and laws allow for discretion, but are heavily regulated; therefore, the flexible desired work environment for Millennials will be a challenge for the proactive police department.

Examples of a challenge

Tax dollars spent to recruit and train police candidates should also be used to retain police officers. Emphasis should be placed on retaining the right person for the community. The financial cost of an officer leaving an agency early in their career is difficult to identify due to the large range of police salaries nationwide. Yet, Millennial-aged employees are not afraid to give their opinion when provided the opportunity. Employers can collect and utilize this data for greater recruitment, satisfaction, and retention. Thus, a research study was performed to determine if police organizations would benefit by identifying factors for Millennial-aged police officers' recruitment, satisfaction, and retention in a Southwest City.

At the time of the study, 28% of police officers employed by the Southwest city were Millennial-aged, born since 1980, with varied amount of tenure. Effective recruitment, selection, and training of police officers were critical due to the aforementioned changing philosophies, expectations, and professionalism of employers and employees. Police academies sent officers to agencies for on-the-job training; essentially to succeed or leave. Millennials were described as the most high-maintenance and high performing generation of employees, yet no stigma existed among their cohort if they quit the job when unhappy. When a young officer decided to leave their employer, police administration did not appropriately address the reasons for the separation through effective exit interviews, if given one at all. To investigate what issues and factors were contributing to attrition rates, we looked at the following four targeted questions.

CHAPTER 17

Themes to Address Millennial Officers Effectively

Questions and Millennial Officers Responses

The four questions asked of Millennial-aged police officers were:

1. What specific factors draw Millennials to work as police officers?
2. What specific workplace factors increase job satisfaction?
3. What specific workplace factors decrease workplace satisfaction?
4. What specific workplace factors promote workplace retention?

Question 1. What specific factors draw Millennials to work as police officers?

The questions produced five general themes critical to the first central question: (a) general excitement, thrill and variety of police work, (b) serve the community and help people, (c) interact with people as a team (d) legacy career – previous family member in policing, and (e) pay and benefits. Each of the themes will be examined and discussed. These following themes appeared from research question number one.

Theme 1. General excitement, thrill and variety of police work

The first theme immediately identified in the first research question was the general excitement, thrill and variety of a career in policing.

This common excitement for a variety of calls appears to resonate throughout the Millennial-aged police officers. They communicated a need to avoid repetition and boredom.

Theme 2. Serving the community and helping people

Theme two suggested Millennial-aged police officers have a philanthropic attitude about policing.

Service to the community was a common comment from the participants. The service aspect of policing appeared to be a deep concept for Millennials to work as police officers.

Theme 3. Interacting with people as a team

Teamwork was a very popular theme for Millennials to come work a policing career. Teamwork was often reported using popular police vernacular such as squads, units, and brotherhood.

The participants all spoke of understanding what it was like to be part of a team throughout the interviews. Teamwork had a deep sense of meaning for the Millennial-aged police officer participants as a factor for obtaining a career in policing.

Theme 4. Legacy career – previous family member in policing

A few of the participants had relatives ranging from parent, grandparent, uncle and cousin as police officers who inspired them to seek law enforcement as a career.

An interesting note is that the relative generally did not recruit the participant to policing, rather the participant looked up to the police relative and wanted to replicate the referent behavior. Legacy policing due to a previous relative in the industry is still a factor for attracting Millennials.

Theme 5. Pay and benefits

Tangible pay and benefits of the job was not left out by Millennials as a factor for seeking policing for employment.

The most mentioned benefits of a policing career were job security and retirement. Mostly, pay referred specifically to starting pay as well as anticipated pay raises as attractive to Millennials.

Summary of Responses to question 1

The findings on what attracts Millennials to work as police officers centered on the excitement for daily work variety of the work environment that a career in law enforcement could provide. Progress and change have become the satisfying factors of job selection and retention of Millennial employees Participants in this study clearly expressed a desire to avoid boredom and office jobs. Excitement for police work must remain novel from the Millennials' perspective. The main theme of workplace novelty of the job also contributed to their sense of service to the community. There were several philanthropic and service-oriented comments that directly identified with the job of a police officer. Millennial-aged police officers want to feel a sense of fulfillment through helping others in the community. Serving the community comes through teamwork for a Millennial. Interaction with the community as a cohesive team supports their service mission. The teamwork aspect within police work gives Millennials a sense of brotherhood and a connection to a work family. Yet, some of the Millennials have previous family members that created a legacy for policing. From immediate to extended family, the policing lifestyle and career was comfortable to some Millennials who were attracted to policing. In addition to the excitement, service, and legacy of police work, Millennials-aged police officers also were attracted to the pay and benefits of the job. The immediate attraction of pay and benefits for the Millennials was often highlighted by the pension at the end of a successful career.

Question 2. What specific workplace factors increase job satisfaction for Millennial-aged police officers?

The analysis of the comments produced five thematic categories critical to the second central question: (a) opportunities for lateral job movement, (b) recognition for work and praise (c) respect for input, new ideas and ways (d) best technology and equipment available, and (e) pay raises as promised when hired. Each of the themes will be examined and discussed. These following themes appeared from research question number two.

Theme 1. Opportunities for Lateral Job Movement

Availability to laterally move around the police department was the first theme identified for research question two. From the Millennial-aged officers' perspectives, and directly in line with the second research question, job opportunities for lateral movement was overwhelmingly a workplace factor that increases job satisfaction.

Comment: *"You can do something different but still have the same job for a significant amount of time....It is almost the same as having a variety of jobs, but it's the same actual career, same employment at every point in time."*

Comment: *"I need to see a few new things in my career. I want to see opportunities to move around or shadow another department, taking a look at what else is out there."*

Comment: *"Opportunities to move through other areas of the department is important....there are lots of things you can do."*

Instead of having multiple jobs like people in other careers, policing provides career mobility for increased job satisfaction by all of the participants. It should be noted that the interviews of Millennial-aged police officers revealed the following words as synonymous with lateral job movement: (a) opportunities, (b) specialties, (c) shadow, (d) options, (e) advancement, (f) transfers, (g) promotion, and (h) mobility. Internal and external motivation was achieved as the participants wanted to avoid a stagnant career by physically moving around the organization and personally enriching their careers.

Theme 2. Recognition for work and praise

Acknowledgement and praise were commonly discussed themes among Millennial-aged police officers for increased workplace satisfaction.

Comment: *"I wanted supervisors and department administration to) let us know we actually matter."*

Comment: *"Awards, (and) appreciation, the Millennials are going to want the appreciation and they want to know why.... Workplace environment is important."*

Comment: *"A balance of right and wrong recognition does not exist".*

Praise and recognition were desired by the participants because of a general negative culture that police officers work in the community and organization. Several of the participants wanted a more positive workplace environment in their negative-heavy law enforcement industry.

Theme 3. Respect for input, new ideas and ways

Receptive input for contemporary ideas and thoughts was a very popular theme form the majority of the Millennial-aged police officers.

Comment: *"We have different thought processes than even our parents or grandparents. As the generations go on, our thought processes change based upon our environments. We have to* change because crime is different than the way it was 20 years ago."

Comment: "(Millennials) are forward thinking and they have good ideas. They are not afraid to voice these ideas. This generation is the now generation"

Comment: "Administration listening better to us would create better satisfaction. Maybe if they came to us for input and then implemented those things we are suggesting." "Just ask for our input and then do something with it. Don't ask if you're not going to do something with it."

The participants also expressed frustration with input received from supervisors and administration that apparently went nowhere. The Millennial-aged officers still understood the rank-and-file system in law enforcement, but identified better feedback of their input would be a factor for increasing workplace satisfaction.

Theme 4. Best technology and equipment available

The latest and greatest technology and police equipment available is a factor for increasing workplace satisfaction.

Comment: "Equipment is everything...to include technology like working computers in your vehicle....we can always do better with technology"

Comment: "I feel like our generation has an understanding of the cyber-culture, like computers, internet-based technologies. I think technology is just one of the biggest parts of what we see nowadays. Most of the crimes I see have some type of internet factor to it".

Comment: "Utilization of technology as an increased satisfier when employers) effectively use technology to make their (Millennials) job more efficient, not necessarily easier."

Comment: "We are more technologically savvy...it is more familiar to us."

Several of the participants referred mobile technology as necessary to fight today's crime.

It appeared Millennials felt negatively judged in their workplace for their technological aptitudes.

Theme 5. Pay raises as promised when hired

Several of the participants stated decisions made before they were hired negatively impacted their merit pay increases. The Millennial-aged officers said they were not looking for extra pay, but wanted the pay they were promised when recruited to become officers. This factor would be both internally and externally satisfying.

Comment: *"Everything is budget related…and we did not get pay raises…it gets discouraging after a while."*

Comment: *"Money after you're here is far more important."*

Comment: *"Want police agencies to keep their promises (regarding pay). My agency is just now catching up on pay raises. I feel like I am expected to keep up my end of the bargain, but maybe they should too."*

Comment: *"This affects your morale. Money is a big thing for people my age, at my age especially we are starting to have a family. Money becomes a factor when you want to buy a house. These are things I did not have to worry about when I started."*

The participants often purposely expressed that they did not enter law enforcement for the money, but hoped to be monetarily satisfied for their time and experience as promised when hired.

Every Millennial-aged police officer interviewed described the importance of a satisfying work environment as very, pretty or extremely important. As with the contemporary literature on Millennial-aged employees, they were unafraid to give input to their organization. Factors for increased workplace satisfaction were clearly presented by the participants. A majority of the Millennial-aged police officers stated if the workplace satisfiers identified in research question number two were absent from their workplace, they would seek employment at another police agency though lateral transfers.

It should be noted that the research was conducted during an economic recession. Assumptions were made regarding pay, benefits, and other budget cuts.

Factors for Increasing Job Satisfaction of Millennial-aged Police Officers

5 Pattern and Themes

1   Opportunities for lateral job movement
2   Recognition for work and praise
3   Respect for input, new ideas and ways
4   Best technology and equipment available
5   Pay raises as promised when hired

Summary of Responses to Question 2

When increasing workplace satisfaction for Millennial-aged officers, opportunities for lateral job movement was a very important finding. As Millennials were attracted to police work for the excitement and variety, increased satisfaction appears to share a similar theme; job mobility. The Millennials expressed a high desire to move around the organization for mainly personal reasons of learning new skills and staying motivated. The participants wanted to avoid a stagnant career in the same job function for too long. As the Millennial-aged officers' careers progress, they clearly want their supervisors and leaders to positively recognize their work. The Millennials explained praise and recognition as a validation for their effort and continued experience. A positive work environment through recognition and praise increases Millennial-aged police officers' workplace satisfaction. According to the participants, the positive workplace environment could also come through a respect from organization leaders about Millennials input and suggestions. The Millennials appeared eager and open to give their opinions in the workplace, and wanted their voices to be heard; to matter such as technology. The best technology and equipment made available to Millennials in the workplace increased their satisfaction and motivation to handle today's police issues. The participants expressed a desire to use technology in most aspects of their careers for greater efficiency. Pay raises as promised when hired was the final finding for increased satisfaction. The Millennial-aged police officers were not asking for additional pay for increased satisfaction, but they were asking the organization to provide them with the pay offered when originally recruited and hired. A Pew Research Center (2010) study identified similar Millennial Generation values, attitudes, and experiences in line with this specific research question.

Question 3: What specific workplace factors decrease workplace satisfaction for Millennial-aged police officers?

The comments revealed three areas critical to the third central question: (a) lack of lateral job movement, (b) micromanaging and poor supervision, and (c) negative police culture. Each of the themes will be examined and discussed. These following themes appeared from question number three.

Theme 1. Lack of lateral job movement

Diminished opportunity of lateral job movement was listed as a major factor for the decreasing workplace satisfaction for Millennial-aged police officers. The lack of mobility was expressed throughout the interviews.

Comment: *"A lot of guys are frustrated with the (lack) of shift change and schedules. We used to do it every year and now we are doing it every two years. A lot of Millennials are getting frustrated because they would eventually like to enjoy a weekend off. The bid is based upon seniority, and now it takes a lot longer to earn it."*

Comment: *"If your department is stagnant, you won't have the ability to go anywhere,"*

Comment: *"We want to learn new things about this job, so I don't feel like I am just doing it again and again day in and day out. Opportunity, while that is starting to come back around, it is not as good as it should be or once was."*

It would seem logical that the absence of lateral movement in an organization would decrease workplace satisfaction because opportunities for movement was viewed as a workplace factor which increased satisfaction. Participants described decreased satisfaction from lack of job movement as stagnation, boredom, and burned out working the same job in the department.

Theme 2. Micromanaging and poor supervision

A majority of the participants identified micromanaging and poor supervision as a workplace factor that decreased satisfaction for Millennial-aged police officers. Poor leadership qualities from their direct supervisors were viewed as a factor for decreased satisfaction.

Comment: *"Maybe they don't value me."*

Comment: *"I want to feel appreciated as an employee."*

Comment: *"Poor supervision. You have guys who are micromanagers. I would say it is more specific to sergeants because they are in line with their staff.... You can actually bid around them or find a way to transfer out, away from them (when lateral job movement is available)."*

Comment: *"The sergeant has the biggest day-to-day impact with us."*

The Millennial-aged officers were very vocal about creating supervisory standards especially at the rank of sergeant. Almost all of the participants used past experiences to reveal what they believed to be the factors that decreased satisfaction. The exact leadership qualities desired by Millennials for their supervisors were not revealed in the research.

Theme 3. Negative police culture

The overall negative police culture was viewed as a factor for decreased satisfaction by the Millennial-aged participants. They felt like administration and supervisors were heavy on the negative communication and almost void of the positive.

Comment: *"The positive and negative affirmation was not balanced… it was heavy on punishment and criticism."*

Comment: *"The negative police culture is disgruntled (police officers). I think there is a reduction in productivity. The feeling like, "Why should I stick my neck out if no one is doing it for me?"*

Comment: *"Hazing can mean a whole lot of things. Not in a sorority/ fraternity kind of way, like they're going to beat our asses, but more like you need to earn your reputation (in the department)….It (occurs) before they work with you. They (other officers and supervisors) make judgements on how you are as a cop."*

Comment: *"The sergeant has the biggest day-to-day impact with us."*

Millennial-aged police officers desired an improved balance between positive and negative feedback at work. All of the Millennial-aged police officers stated they are currently or had experienced the identified factors that decrease workplace satisfaction. More importantly, all but one of the participants knew of several officers who are currently leaving the organization or quit a police career altogether due to workplace factors decreasing satisfaction.

Factors for Decreasing Job Satisfaction of Millennial-aged Police Officers

3 Patterns and Themes

1   Lack of lateral job movement
2   Micromanaging and poor supervision
3   Negative police culture

Summary of Responses to Question 3

The findings for factors that decrease workplace satisfaction for Millennial-aged police officers immediately identified a lack of lateral job movement. This research found Millennial employees behaved differently in the workplace, because most employers seemingly failed to integrate the needs of these successive generations. Through a recession and organizational attrition, the ability to move around the police department to different specialties and units had been stifled for several years.

The lack of workplace variety and the stimulus related to novelty, the participants shared a decreased workplace satisfaction. This decreased satisfaction was exacerbated by their perception of micromanaging supervisors. The Millennial-aged officers believed poor supervision reduced workplace satisfaction. The participants also stated a lack of perceived value for their work was communicated by some supervisors. The Millennials clearly pointed out that not all supervisors acted this way, but those who did were avoided during time to bid or transfer around the department. The Millennials believed poor supervision added to the overall negative police culture. A negative police culture was described as a workplace environment heavy on punishment and criticism and light on positive affirmation and praise.

Question 4: What specific workplace factors promote workplace retention for Millennial-aged police officers?

The data analysis produced five thematic categories critical to the fourth central question: (a) opportunities for lateral job movement, (b) increased recognition and praise (c) leadership development for sergeants, (d) pay raises as promised, and (e) increased vertical communication. Each of the themes will be examined and discussed. These following themes appeared from research question number four.

Theme 1. Increased opportunities for movement

The stagnation felt by the Millennial-aged participants often carried through the entire interview. It was very apparent that Millennials desire constant stimulus and novelty.

Comment: *"Having the opportunity to move and grow (was the most important factor for retention). I want the opportunity... Some people are willing to stay in patrol their whole careers. I think other Millennials feel exactly the same. They want to move to criminal investigations, K-9, court officers, narcotics, (and) under cover....Maybe chief one day."*

Comment: *"Millennials must continue to provide opportunities....this is the generation who is coming up and who will eventually be the new leaders....we need to keep moving forward."*

Comment: *"The ability to move around the department...invest in the employee...send them to training...show them you want them here."*

All of the participants shared stories of friends and coworkers who have or are currently considering leaving the organization due to a lack of opportunity to move laterally in the department. Several of the participants had requested employment information from or applied to other police organizations. Some of the participants were not selected by the other agencies while others changed their minds and stayed with their current agency.

Theme 2. Increased Recognition and praise:

Millennial-aged police officers desire recognition and praise for their work from their direct supervisors and administration.

Comment: *"Leaders to communicate positive affirmation while holding them accountable."*

Comment: *"The main thing would be to know that my organization has my back. Obviously, not if I violate policy. But, if I do*

> *what is needed to do, to stay within policy, I want to know they have my back. I would think they (administration) would want to keep us happy so we feel motivated to get up and go to work to get things accomplished."*

Comment: *"If you have a high-performing Millennial (provide) constructive criticism, and invest in them so they feel like they are a contributing member."*

Comment: *"Make everyone feel like they have a vested interest".*

Participants believed they were doing the same noble profession as their superiors, yet rarely received positive feedback. The perception of negative recognition appeared to greatly outweigh the positive, according to the Millennials. Positive recognition and praise from supervisors and administration clearly was a factor for the retention of Millennial-aged police officers.

Theme 3. Leadership development for sergeants:

Specific leadership training to standardize sergeants' actions across the department was a consistent theme to retain Millennial-aged police officers.

Comment: *"Supervision kept Millennials bottled up and not able to live up to their greatest potential."*

Comment: *"Good supervisors who always have the "good job mindset," are so good at positive reinforcement and they make you fell worthy and wanted. Trust them (Millennials). The ability to let a Millennial go out, give them direction as to what you want them to do and trust them to go out and do it. If you are going to give them a task, let them do it right or wrong – without being up their rears…help them learn from it.…This will continue to build your agency from the bottom, it will keep it new, it will bring new ideas."*

Comment: *"Some supervisors are great, but some feel like they have to be babysitters…they now feel like they have to control everything."*

Participants referenced back to previous questions and discussed a need for more trust and less micromanagement from the direct supervisors as a factor that promotes workplace retention. Leadership development for sergeants was a factor listed by Millennial-aged police officers which promotes workplace retention.

Theme 4. Pay raises as promised

Participants did not overtly complain or request more pay or benefits. However, the Millennial-aged police officers greatly desired the pay and benefits promised when they were recruited and hired.

Comment: *"I want progressive pay for (my) experience."*
Comment: *"Bring back step-pay increases prior to the current budget freeze."*
Comment: *"It was pretty rough with the budgets, (but) you also need to get paid…maintain the benefits you're promised when you come in, that needs to be done."*

Participants felt less appreciated than previous employees even though they understood the recession impacted the current budgets. A consistent theme was pay and benefits - as promised by the organization when hired.

Theme 5. Increased vertical communication

The Millennial-aged police officers considered themselves diverse communicators with today's technological advances. Yet, they want more effective vertical communication from their entire supervision chain of command.

Comment: *"It is imperative to have a police department who can communicate and connect with those people (Millennials)."*
Comment: *"Older folks get stuck in their thoughts and ways, you want a fresh outlook to mix it up, but the input must be received (by the supervisor)."*

Comment: "Vertical communication from supervisors and administration would be better than relying on a post on social
media from other Millennials."

Supervisors and administration valuing Millennials' input and
communication while offering "why" something is or is not implemented describes increased vertical communication according to
the participants. The terms "open lines of communication" and
"open-door policy" were commonly discussed by the participants as
important for workplace retention.

Factors for Retaining Millennial-aged Police Officers

5 Patterns and Themes

1   Opportunities for lateral job movement
2   Increased recognition and praise
3   Leadership development for sergeants
4   Pay raises as promised
5   Increased vertical communication

Summary of Responses to Question 4

The factors that promoted retention of Millennial-aged police officers
pointed directly to increased opportunities for lateral job movement.
Desire to move around and experience new jobs in the organization
were extremely important to the participants, including opportunities
to shadow another unit of department.

Increased positive recognition and praise for their work were
desired by the participants. Millennials stated they rarely received
positive feedback for their work, which reduced personal value and in
turn negatively affects workplace retention. Therefore, Millennial-aged
police officers were looking for validation in their organizations
through positive recognition and praise.

Efforts must be made to retain the best talent. Participants said the first-line supervisors should be provided leadership development training to increase Millennial retention. Their hope was a supervision standard for sergeants through leadership training to create a better work environment.

Receiving pay raises as promised would retain the Millennial-aged police officers. Millennials only asked for the pay and benefits offered when recruited and hired to be fully restored. The Millennials often made suggestions and felt ignored by administration due to lack of implementation of their input. The participants asked the organizational leaders to communicate why something was or was not implemented so they know they were heard; valued. This process may be possible through increased vertical communication throughout the ranks.

Themes

The impact of a police culture with low satisfaction and morale can be devastating to the officers, organization and the community in which they serve. Police officer turnover, absenteeism, and low productivity negatively affect community taxpayers and the delivery of public safety service. Millennial employees are fast-paced, technologically proficient, and change-oriented. Identifying factors and experiences that improve workplace satisfaction among Millennial-aged police officers is paramount for the future of policing.

The 13 themes identified can and will assist police leaders in identifying and developing the best organizational environments to address Millennial employees more effectively.

To summarize the themes obtained through the questions asked of Millennial aged officers the following should be noted:

1. General excitement, the thrill and variety of police work
2. Wanting to serve the community and help people.
3. Interact with people as a team.
4. Legacy career – previous family member in policing.

5. Excellent pay and benefits.
6. Opportunities for lateral job task movement.
7. Recognition for work and praise.
8. Respect for their input and new ideas.
9. The best technology and equipment available.
10. Avoiding micromanagement and poor supervision.
11. Leadership development opportunities for sergeants.
12. Avoiding a negative police culture.
13. Increased vertical chain of command communication.

CHAPTER 18

Workplace Suggestions for Improved Millennial-aged Police Officer Satisfaction

To recruit Millennials into government service, police departments must offer opportunities for innovation, serving others, and flexible environments to best use their talents. Millennials are optimistic, and have big expectations, but they do not believe they will have a career with just one employer. After hiring, training and satisfaction of employee retention should be the main focus for police leaders.

As discussed before, flexible work arrangements and opportunities to serve society are more important to Millennial police applicants than the initial size of the pay/benefits package. It is unclear what this type of work environment would look like in the current police industry. Since police work is a boots-on-the-ground career that requires human attention, it requires specific action and intervention.

Millennials are described as optimistic about their employment future, but they believe that they will have many jobs and possibly many careers. Knowing Millennials believe they will have many jobs, organizations should market policing as many different jobs within the same career and organization. For example, police recruiters could solicit Millennials for a police career by laying out the different police careers such as community service through patrol, investigations, public information, and neighborhood outreach as well as offer flexibility through shift changes and rotating assignments. Police roles may offer a lateral transfer while maintaining a steady income, possible pay raises, and a single retirement without changing employers or having to start over. If the Millennial applicant does not expect to have a career with one employer, then perhaps recruiting them by emphasizing all of the careers within a single organization would prove beneficial. Opportunities within the same organization now become attractive multiple jobs without losing an employee who has to start over.

Police departments nationwide have reported difficulty filling available positions, but the number of qualified applicants has not decreased even though the Millennials are currently the largest generation in the American workforce. Creative recruiting styles and venues specifically selected for Millennials could be explored by police departments beyond the traditional military and college job fairs to community and gaming events. With the impending exit of baby boomer employees in the future, open-minded management will attract the best Millennial employees. Creating a flexible recruiting atmosphere at unique venues could attract the best Millennial employees for police work, because traditional recruiting tactics are no longer working. Creative police recruiters and leaders could look to nontraditional venues with target-rich environments for recruitment such as video game conferences, sporting events and spring-breakers to best fill the police vacancies with Millennial-aged applicants.

A Pew Research Center study of Millennial culture discussed life cycle effects, period effects, and cohort effects on their environment. In their life cycle, parents and media continuously impact their worldviews. During their formative years, Millennials develop a sense of self and decide to give back to their society based upon their experiences. All people with access to modern western media have life cycle effects that are shared by a generation. Older generations were shaped during their formative years and may fail to recognize or appreciate the life cycle effects of millennial-aged police officers.

This lack of understanding will cause conflict. Learning about the formative years and life cycle of Millennials will improve supervisor and coworker interpersonal relationships.

As with all generations, adolescence to teenager and adult cause dramatic changes in our lives. Environmental factors that occur during each period of life transition will affect an individual. For example, a Millennial teenager whose parents were divorced shortly after the terrorist attacks of September 11, 2001 may be greatly impacted during this exact period as opposed to a younger Millennial who learned about 9/11 years later in a history class. Personal and environmental events that can coincide with important periods in life may develop differing world views. A brief pre-hire interview could allow a police recruiter to communicate more effectively with the Millennial candidate to best meet their employment needs through identification of strong period effects. A similar approach could be used by police trainers and supervisors to identify personal satisfiers from their formative years.

Cohort effects are experiences generally shared across the entire generation. Increased technological speed and dependence, worldwide wars, and political scandals all shared across the Millennial Generation will develop similar worldviews. An entire generation may have similar opinions on certain topics based upon this cohort effect, and the Millennial Generation is prepared to make their unique impression on the America. Training for police leaders regarding historical Millennial cohort effects could reduce current frustrations and anxiety that cause organizational conflict.

A positive relationship has been reported between quality performance by the leader and commitment by their followers. Police leaders who create and maintain positive relationships with Millennial officers will have greater influence on these followers. Therefore, a more supportive culture modeled by optimistic senior personnel is important to morale, whereas non-modeling has a negative impact. Competency, organizational context, leader performance, and follower commitment among police officers is connected to the established relationship, as the leaders' psychological capital positively relates to follower performance in policing.

Collaborative police environments may find greater acceptance from Millennial officers. Assessing officers' needs and assigning responsibility without assessing blame is a contemporary tactic in policing. Addressing shortcomings and failures as opportunities for learning and growth are much more effective workplace environments for the Millennial officer.

Application of contemporary business management and leadership principles to policing could affect positive change. Leaders need to teach and train the Millennial-aged officers to manage themselves internal to the greater police culture. The development of a new organizational culture and positive climate in policing is emphasized for greater effectiveness. As an example, the new concept of part-time policing could be offered as a flexible way to maintain employee satisfaction and retain talent. A paradigm shift in current police philosophies is necessary to positively influence Millennial-aged officers toward greater workplace satisfaction.

Anthropological police history combined with sociological generational differences amplifies the individual police psychological behaviors and communication styles. Understanding the differences in communication styles is paramount to a healthy and successful law enforcement career.

Multiple generations are working together in every profession in the United States. The communication challenges and efforts by each of these generations, at times, appears challenging. A conscious effort to identify what makes each generational cohort unique in the workplace will, no doubt, improve employee satisfaction and retention.

James R. DeLung, Ph.D.

Appendix A
Police Personality Research

Concern with the quality of American policing and police dates back roughly to 1931 and the publication of the findings of the Wickersham Commission. This commission produced the first systematic explanation of the American criminal justice system. While the explanation centered on routine police practices, the report encouraged further research by people who today would call themselves criminologists.

The concerns and research seemed to focus on what makes up a law enforcement officer; and in knowing how the officer may function, how can we better understand and direct police behavior? Scholars started to gather data, and gather they did! In the late 1950s through the early 1960s, numerous studies were conducted in the profession. Peter Manning, a criminologist and researcher, listed over 78 various police research projects being conducted in 1976 alone, the era considered as the "Golden Age of Police Research." It was interesting to note, however, that research on police personality involving the use of the Myers-Briggs Type Indicator® (MBTI) didn't surface until 1978.

Wayne B. Hanewicz was the first major researcher to publish using the Jungian conceptual framework of personality types for the law enforcement profession. He used the MBTI framework to categorize various traits displayed by police officers into the sixteen types defined by the Myers-Briggs Type Indicator. Hanewicz defined personality according to sociologist Thomas C. Gray's (1975) notion of affinity: "...a predisposition to adhere partially to a set of distinctive sentiments that can be expanded and reinforced by training and socialization."

Hanewicz interpreted previous research as reflecting two major positions: first, the police personality is something police possess by being police, (i.e., job related) and, secondly, the police personality is something inherent in people who choose to become police officers. In the first case, "police personality" refers to a group of traits that are acquired after employment and is characteristic of the police profession alone. In the second case, "police personality" signifies a group of traits common to, but not exclusive of, police officers. Using this definition, a person who enters the police profession may share common characteristics with a person who enters another field which stresses some of the same traits needed to do police work.

Many researchers felt there was a personality exclusive to police, but Hanewicz disagreed, taking into consideration the Myers-Briggs instrument, Carl Jung's theory, and other studies. Hanewicz and others felt there were possible overlaps between the personality required for police work and some other jobs.

According to Hanewicz, Jungian typology represented a promising approach to investigating the commonalities between police work and other occupations. He described a study undertaken with the Miami, Florida, police department to improve police-citizen inter-action. Determinants of police behavior were studied to understand the factors which influence police behavior and to relate them to police functions.

In the study, psychiatrist Jesse Rubin is quoted as saying, "The type of people who enter police work are generally psychologically healthy and competent young men who display common personality features that should serve them well in a police career." He described them as generally restless and assertive, with a high level of physical energy. Further, their restlessness seems to derive from an aversion to introspection; rather, "policemen look to the environment for perceptual stimulation in order to maintain alertness and optimal functioning."

Hanewicz also quoted a study of the New York City Police Department training activities, funded by the National Institute of Law Enforcement and Criminal Justice, which compared the value dimensions of police recruits entering the department in 1959 and again in 1968. He found a remarkable similarity among the personality traits valued by the recruits in both years, even though they were a decade apart. Alertness, job knowledge, honesty, dedication, and common sense were the top five of forty possible choices in the 1959 group, and were among the top six in the 1968 group.

Hanewicz's conclusions concentrated primarily on the predominance of certain personality styles in the police profession and the fact these personality traits were shared by police along with those in certain other occupations. However, he only touched on the various possible organizational implications Jungian typology suggests in better understanding the law enforcement profession.

Several other researchers also examined police personality through the use of the MBTI. Ron Cacioppe and Philip Mock, two researchers from Australia, conducted a study on police self-actualization, quality of work experience, and stress. The personality type distribution in their sample of 191 senior Australian police resembled that of Hanewicz.

Another researcher, Ronald Lynch, who was with the Institute of Government at the University of North Carolina, conducted several studies involving the use of the Myers-Briggs Type Indicator®. Lynch found the distribution of the various Jungian types throughout the police profession was much the same as the distribution Hanewicz found. Lynch also commented on the fact that the tasks of policing were also common to other occupations as well, such as banking and engineering.

Hobart M. Henson, a Deputy Director with the Illinois State Police, conducted a comprehensive study utilizing the MBTI, seeking to develop criteria to help in recruiting persons especially suited to be police officers and to more effectively select, train, motivate, and plan for growth in his agency. His data, drawn from a comprehensive sample of 2,114 veteran and recruit police officers, indicated the same general distribution of personality types according to the MBTI as did Hanewicz and Lynch.

The type distributions from the studies of Wayne Hanewicz, Hobart Henson, and Ron Lynch, along with the studies conducted by Hennessy and others with three hundred police executives, resulted in a Composite Police Profile according to Jungian cognitive styles of taking in information and making decisions. As one can see from the following percentages, the Intuitive Feeling (NF) cognitive style is least represented in law enforcement. The majority of police personnel clearly prefer the Sensing Thinking (ST) cognitive style.

	Police	General Population*
Sensing Thinking Style	65 – 70 %	32-42 %
Intuitive Thinking Style	14 %	15 – 22 %
Sensing Feeling Style	11 %	31 – 41 %
Intuitive Feeling Style	15 – 21 %	5%

* From Estimated Frequencies of the Types in the United States Population by C. R. Martin, 1996. Gainesville, FL: Center for Applications of Psychological Type

Note that about 50 percent of the individuals who make up Jungian cognitive norms prefer making decisions (Judgment) with the use of the Feeling function, while only 20 percent of the police prefer making decisions in that manner.

Appendix B
Development of the Law Enforcement Personality Profile®

During my years of research with the Myers Briggs Type Instrument®, the development of a more specific personality profile for those in the law enforcement and public safety profession made sense. To help individuals in the profession to better understand how important the need for better communication in the police profession through the lens of Carl Jung's theories of personality type, Dr. Hennessy began to develop the instrument that was police profession specific.

The instrument was designed to measure the Cognitive Functions of Carl Jung's theories which are the taking in of information (Perception) and the making of decisions (Judgment). Not included were other measures such as Extraversion and Introversion or Judgment and Perception which are important, but for the specific instrument, were not deemed necessary to understand general communication patterns.

Several thousand police personnel and those in related professions have taken the Profile to date. Comparing the results to other instruments measuring the same Jungian Cognitive Styles indicate that the Law Enforcement Personality profile °very consistent with the results of other assessments.

A 60-item questionnaire was designed using a police specific vocabulary. Of the 60 items, 30 questions measure Perception or taking in of information and 30 measure Judgment or decision making. Of the 30 questions on Perception, 15 were designed to measure the sensing function and 15 to measure the intuitive function. Of the 30 questions on Judgment, 15 were designed to reflect the Thinking (pure logic) function and 15 to measure the Feeling (social value or people orientation) function.

The instrument takes approximately 15 minutes to complete and is in a self-scorable version, Participants can score their own responses. A Power-Point with presentational instructions is furnished along with the assessment.

On completion, the participants will have a dominant style of police personality. The participants then exchange the reusable question booklet and receive an 8-page Description Booklet that describes their personality style in more detail, along with descriptions of the three other styles prevalent in the law enforcement profession. The profile can be found at www.law-enforcement-personality-profile.com.

Stephen M. Hennessy, Ed.D.

Appendix C
Research on Generational Styles of Policing

The research examined was the perceived low workplace satisfaction among Millennial-aged police officers. Current police workplace research indicated the problem may be a Millennial Generation issue rather than a systemic law enforcement concern. Failure to address this problem and identify the perception of workplace satisfaction for Millennial-aged police officers serves to maintain the current negative morale present in police culture. Maintaining low satisfaction as status quo for future policing generations is negative for all communities. Contemporary peer-reviewed literature and popular media sources reported Millennial employee work behavior as wearisome to employers.

Millennials reported that they would like to have long careers with the same employer, but they do not believe this to be a viable option in today's world. This research identified workplace issues affecting the morale and satisfaction of Millennial-aged police officers. Findings will assist police executives with current and future employment decisions to improve the quality of internal and external service. Millennials appeared to measure success by enjoying what they are doing and consider job satisfaction as important as pay and benefits. Identifying specific Millennial-aged police motivators through Herzberg's Two-Factor Theory provided specific indicators of workplace satisfaction for organizational leaders to implement. This research explored new ways of satisfying police officers in a rigid, old-guard style of management commonly found in policing which dissatisfies Millennial-aged officers.

Communities demand high-quality service from their police officers, and police leaders must integrate the workplace satisfaction needs of succeeding generations, and this research specifically explored the Millennial-aged police-officer satisfaction problem in an attempt to close the gap in the research. All factors identified by the participants were collected and examined.

The purpose of this research was to examine perceptions of workplace satisfaction through the shared experiences of Millennial-aged police officers. Researching the perceptions of workplace satisfaction for Millennial-aged police officers identified specific motivators that leaders may implement to positively affect their organizations. When Millennials discuss important job characteristics, they were unafraid to give candid responses; therefore interpersonal interviews were used in the research. Examination of the research findings from these individual interviews of Millennial-aged officers may greatly benefit leaders as they develop satisfying workplace environments for future generations.

James R. DeLung, Ph.D.

References

Alsop, R. (2008). The trophy kids grow up. San Francisco, CA: Jossey-Bass.

Altes, K. (2009, Sep-Oct). Social media: Young professionals effect change in the workplace [Journal]. Journal of Property Management, 44-47. Retrieved from http://search.proquest.com.proxy1.ncu.edu

Archbold, C. A. (2013). The history of the police. In Policing. Los Angeles, CA: Sage.

Arizona Peace Officer Standards and Training Board [AZPOST]. (n.d.). Retrieved from http://www.azpost.state.az.us/

Aryafar, M. K., & Ezzedeem, S. R. (2008). [Review of the book The trophy kids grow up: How the Millennial generation is shaking up the workplace, by R. Alsop]. Retrieved from http://search.proquest.com.proxy1.ncu.edu

Balda, J. B., & Mora, F. (2011). Adapting leadership theory and practice for the networked, Millennial generation. Journal of Leadership Studies, 5(3), 13-24. http://dx.doi.org/10.1002/jls.20229

Bannon, S., Ford, K., & Meltzer, L. (2011, November). Understanding Millennials in the workplace [Journal]. The CPA Journal, 61-65. Retrieved from http://search.proquest.com.proxy1.ncu.edu

Basu, I. (2012). Social media elevates community policing. Retrieved from http://www.govtech.com/dc/articles/Social-Media-Elevates-Community-Policing.html

Barford, I. N., & Hester, P. T. (2011, March-April). Analyzing generation y workforce motivation. Defense AT&L, 36-40. Retrieved from http://search.proquest.com.proxy1.ncu.edu

Behrens, W. (2009, Spring). Managing Millennials: They're coming to a workplace near you [Journal]. Marketing Health Services, 19-21. Retrieved from http://search.proquest.com.proxy1.ncu.edu

Borges, N. J., Manuel, R. S., Elam, C. L., & Jones, B. J. (2010). Differences in motives between Millennial and generation x medical students [Journal]. Medical Education, 44, 570-576. Retrieved from http://search.proquest.com.proxy1.ncu.edu

Bristow, M. S. (2011, January 3). Make way for generation y [Newsgroup comment]. Retrieved from http://finance.yahoo.com/career-work/article/111715/make-way-for-generation-y

Cacioppe, Ron L., and Mock, Philip (1985). Developing the police officer at work. Leadership and Organizational Development Journal, 6, 5.

Cappitelli, P. (2014). 3 ways to combat degradation of morale in your agency. Retrieved from http://www.policeone.com/police-leader/article s/7530773-3-ways-to-combat-degradation-of-morale-in-your-agency/

Cates, S. V. (2010, August). Generational management in corporate America: The differences and challenges in management of four generations of working adults. Chinese Business Review, 9, 46-54. Retrieved from http://www.academia.edu/1395671/Generational_management_in_corporate_America_The_differences_and_challenges_in_management_of_four_generations_of_working_adults

Cekada, T. L. (2012, March). Training a multigenerational workforce. Professional Safety, 57(3), 40-44. Retrieved from http://www.asse.org/professionalsafety/pastissues/057/03/040_044_F1Cekada_0312.pdf

Center for the Application of Psychological Type (CAPT) Gainesville, Florida.

Chapman, R., & Scheider, M. C. (n.d.). Community policing: Now more than ever. Retrieved from http://www.cops.usdoj.gov/default. asp?Item=716

Chappell, A. T., & Lanza-Kaduce, L. (2009, December 29). Police academy socialization: Understanding the lessons learned in a paramilitary-bureaucratic organization [Journal]. Journal of Contemporary Ethnography, 1-28. doi: 10.1177/0891241609342230

Clare, C. (2009, September-October). Generational differences: Turning challenges into opportunities. Journal of Property Management, 40-43. Retrieved from http://search.proquest.com. proxy1.ncu.edu

Cogin, J. (2012, June). Are generational differences in work values fact or fiction? Multi-country evidence and implications. The International Journal of Human Resource Management, 23(11), 2268-2294. Retrieved from http://dx.doi.org/10.1080/09585192. 2011.610967

Cruickshank, D. (2013, September). Recognizing the true cost of low morale. The Police Chief. Retrieved from http://www.police-chiefmagazine.org

Crumpacker, M., & Crumpacker, J. M. (2007, Winter). Succession planning and generational stereotypes: Should HR consider age-based values and attitudes a relevant factor or a passing fad? [Journal]. Public Personnel Management, 36(4), 349-358. Retrieved from http:://search.proquest.com.proxy1.ncu.edu

DeLung, James R. (2015). Examination of Factors for Workplace Satisfaction of Millennial-aged Police Officers. http://gateway.proquest.com/openurl?url_ver=Z39.88-2004&res_dat=xri:pqdiss&rft_val_fmt=info:ofi/fmt:kev:mtx:dissertation&rft_dat=xri:pqdiss:3708832

Dunlap, J. (2014). The 20 most awesome company offices. Retrieved from http://www.incomediary.com/top-20-most-awesome-company-offices

Ekblad, A., & Hathaway, T. (2010, September/October). Working with generation Y [Magazine]. Exchange, 90-93. Retrieved from http://search.proquest.com.proxy1.ncu.edu

Eldridge, L. (2012, September 13). The 'me generation' and the future of law enforcement. PoliceOne.com News. Retrieved from http://www.policeone.com

Emeagwali, N. S. (2011, May). Millennials: leading the charge for change [Journal]. Techniques: Connecting Education & Careers, 22-26. Retrieved from http://search.proquest.com.proxy1.ncu.edu

Emelo, R. (2011, May). What if Millennials ran your mentoring program? Chief Learning Officer, 32-36. Retrieved from http://search.proquest.com.proxy1.ncu.edu

Etter, Sr., G., & Griffin, R. (2010, March 4). In-service training of older law enforcement officers: An andragogical argument. Policing: An International Journal of Police Strategies & Management, 34(2), 233-245. http://dx.doi.org/101108/13639511111148861

Ferri-Reed, J. (2010, April). The keys to engaging Millennials. The Journal for Quality & Participation, 31-33. Retrieved from http://search.proquest.com.proxy1.ncu.edu

Frisbee, George R. (1988). Cognitive styles: An alternative to Keirsey's temperaments. Journal of Psychological Type, 16, 13- 21.

Gentry, W. A., Griggs, T. L., Deal, J. J., Mondore, S. P., & Cox, B. D. (2011, January). A comparison of generational differences in endorsement of leadership practices with actual leadership skill level [Journal]. American Psychological Association, 63(1), 39-49. doi: 10.1037/a0023015

Goldstein, Herman (1977). Policing a free society. Cambridge, MA: Ballinger Publishing.

Gray, Thomas C. (1975). Selecting for a police subculture. In Jerome H. Skolnick and Thomas C. Gray (Eds.), Police in America. Boston, MA: Educational Associates.

Greengard, S. (2011, May/June). Managing a multigenerational workforce [Journal]. CIO Insight, 22-25. Retrieved from http://search.proquest.com.proxy1.ncu.edu

Hammill, G. (2005, Winter/Spring). Mixing and managing four generations of employees. FDU Magazine Online. Retrieved from http://www.fdu.edu/newspubs/magazine/05ws/generations.htm

Hanewicz, Wayne B. (1978, April). Police personality: A Jungian perspective. Crime and Delinquency, 24, 2, 152-172.

Hennessy, Stephen M. (1992). A study of uncommon Myers-Briggs cognitive styles in law enforcement (Doctoral dissertation, University of St. Thomas, St. Paul, 1990). Dissertation Abstracts International, 52/12, 4308A. (University Microfilms No. AAC92-11842).

Hennessy, Stephen M. (1997, December). Multicultural awareness training structure with Arizona police recruits. Crime & Justice International, 9-11.

Hennessy, Stephen M., Warring, D. E, Arnott, J. S., Cornett-DeVito, M. M., & Heuett, G. H. (1998). A cultural awareness trainer's manual for law enforcement officers. Scottsdale, AZ: Leadership Inc.

Hennessy, Stephen M. "Cultural Sensitivity Training" 2nd Ed. (2000) Chapter 12, in James E. Hendricks and Bryan Byers, Eds. Multicultural Perspectives in Criminal Justice and Criminology, Charles Thomas Publishing, Springfield, Ill.

Hennessy, Stephen M. "Cultural Awareness Training for Police in the United States" Chapter 6, in Enhancing Intercultural Competence in Police Organizations (2002) Leenen, W. R. (ed) Műnster; Berlin, D.E., New York, N.Y.

Hennessy, Stephen M. Racial Profiling (2002) Foreword for book by Darin Fredrickson and Raymond P. Siljander, Charles C. Thomas Publishing, Illinois, Springfield

Henson, Hobart M. (1984). A study in police personality in a major police organization. Unpublished study of the Illinois State Police, Springfield, Illinois.

Hewlett, S. A., Sherbin, L., & Sumberg, K. (2009, July-August). How gen Y & boomers will reshape your agenda [Journal]. Harvard Business Review, 71-76. Retrieved from http://search.proquest.com.proxy1.ncu.edu

Hira, N. A. (2007, May 28). You raised them, now manage them [Magazine]. Fortune, 155(10), 38-44. Retrieved from http://search.ebscohost.com.proxy1.ncu.edu

Hirsh, Sandra, and Kummerow, Jean (1987). Introduction to type in organizations. Palo Alto, CA: Consulting Psychologists Press.

Howe, N., & Strauss, W. (2007, July-August). The next 20 years: How customer and workforce attitudes will evolve. Harvard Business Review, 41-52. Retrieved from https://hbr.org/2007/07/the-next-20-years-how-customer-and-workforce-attitudes-will-evolve

Hulett, K. J. (2006, November/December). They are here to replace us: Recruiting and retaining Millennials [Journal]. Solutions, 17. Retrieved from http://search.proquest.com.proxy1.ncu.edu

Johnson, A. (2011, April). From the mouth of Ys [Journal]. Chartered Accountants Journal, 28-29. Retrieved from http://search.proquest.com.proxy1.ncu.edu

Jung, Carl G. (1974). Psychological types (R. F C. Hull Translation). Zurich: Rascher Verlag (Original work published 1921).

Kaifi, B., Nafei, W., Khanfar, N., & Kaifi, M. (2012, November 28). A milt-generational workforce: Managing and understanding Millennials. International Journal of Business and Management, 7(24), 88-93. http://dx.doi.org/10.5539/ijbm.v7n24p88

Kania, R. (2004, February 1). A brief history of a venerable paradigm in policing. Journal of Contemporary Justice, 20, 80-83. http://dx.doi.org/10.1177/1043986203262311

Lancaster, L. C., & Stillman, D. (2010). Millennial nation. In The m factor: How the Millennial generation is rocking the workplace (pp. 3-16). New York, NY: HaperCollins.

Lester, S., Standifer, R., Schultz, N., & Windsor, J. (2012, July 5). Actual versus perceived generational differences at work: An empirical examination. Journal or Leadership & Organizational Studies, 19(3), 341-354. http://dx.doi.org/10.1177/1548051812442747

Libicer, S. R. (2013, May/June). Bring back qualitative policing. National Academy Associate, 14-19.

Lublin, N. (2010). In defense of Millennials [Magazine]. Fast Company, 149, 72-73. Retrieved from http://search.edscohost.com/login.aspx?direct=true&db=buh&AN=53731602&site=ehost-live

Lynch, Ronald G. (1986). The police manager. New York, NY: Random House.

MacDonald, H.A. The Ferguson Effect.

Manning, Peter (1976). The researcher: An alien in the police world. In Arthur Neiderhoffer and Abraham S. Blumberg (Eds.), The ambivalent force. Hinsdale, IL: The Dryden Press.

Macdaid, Gerald P., McCaulley, Mary H., & Kainz, Richard I. (1986). Atlas of type tables. Gainesville, FL: Center for Applications of Psychological Type.

Mannheim, K. (1936). Ideology and utopia. [Google Books]. Retrieved from http://books.google.com/books?hl=en&lr=&id=NxethJLLfGoC&oi=fnd&pg=PR11&dq=ideology+and+utopia&ots=SAifnspl9d&sig=3qNMI40wQFcIgTBhDTaTYqmVKgI#v=onepage&q=ideology%20and%20utopia&f=false

Martin, Charles R. (1996). Estimated frequencies of the types in the United States population. Gainesville, FL: Center for Applications of Psychological Type.

Massey, M. (2006). What you are is where you were when... again! [DVD]. Cambridge, MA: Enterprise Media

McCaulley, Mary H. (1990). The Myers-Briggs Type Indicator and leadership. In K. E. Clark and M. B. Clark (Eds.), Measures of leadership. West Orange, NJ: Leadership Library of America, Inc.

Myers, Isabel Briggs (1976). Myers-Briggs Type Indicator, Form G. Palo Alto, CA: Consulting Psychologists Press.

Myers, Isabel Briggs, and McCaulley, Mary H. (1985). Manual: A guide to the development and use of the Myers-Briggs Type Indicator. Palo Alto, CA: Consulting Psychologists Press.

Neighborhood Watch. (2015). Retrieved from http://www.ncpc.org/topics/home-and-neighborhood-safety/neighborhood-watch

Orrick, D. (2013, August). Toxic personalities. Law and Order, 60-61.

Patterson, J. (1995). Community policing: Learning the lessons of history. Retrieved from http://www.lectlaw/files/cjs07.htm

Police culture and behavior. Unpublished manuscript. (2005). Retrieved from http://faculty.ncwc.edu/mstevens/205/205lect02

Potter, G. (2013). The history of policing in the United States. Retrieved from http://www.plsonline.eku.edu/sites/plsonline.eku.edu/files/the-history-of-policing-in-us.pdf

Ralston, E. S., & Chadwick, S. A. (2009, December). An empirical exploration of the dimensionality of inter-employee trust in police organizations. Policing: An International Journal of Police Strategies & Management, 33(3), 431-451. http://dx.doi.org/10.1108/13695110011066845

Rubin, Jesse G. (1974). Police identity and the police role. In Jack Goldsmith and Sharon S. Goldsmith (Eds.), The police community: Dimensions of an occupational subculture. Pacific Palisades, CA: Palisades Publishing.

Scaramella, G., Cox, S., & McCamey, W. (2010). The police culture. In Introduction to Policing (pp. 97-124). Retrieved from http://sagepub.com/upm-data/38432_4.pdf

Sanders, Charles B., Jr. (1970). Police education and training: Key to better law enforcement. Washington, DC: Brookings Institute.

Sharp, K. (2012, July). Generational conflict in the workplace: From overtime to authority, there really is middle ground. Law and Order, 52-57.

Siegfried, Jr., R. L. (2008, November). Mapping a career path for attracting & retaining talent [Journal]. Financial Executive, 52-55. Retrieved from http://search.proquest.com.proxy1.ncu.edu

Silent Witness. (2015). http://www.silentwitness.org/

Simons, N. (2010, January/February). Leveraging generational work styles to meet business objectives. Information Management, 28-33. Retrieved from http://search.proquest.com.proxy1.ncu.edu

Singer, June (1973). Boundaries of the soul: A primer of Jung's psychology. Garden City, NY: Anchor Press.

Szoltysik, C. (Producer). (2014, August 25). AZ POST Millennial Officer Stat Request. Retrieved from http://www.azpost.gov

Taylor, P., & Keeter, S. (Ed.). (2010). Millennials: A portrait of generation next. Retrieved from Pew Research Center: http://pewsocialtrends.org/files/2010/10/Millennials-confident-connected-open-to-change.pdf

Trulock, H. (2011, August 9). The Millennial generation: Do you fit the mold? [Student Branding Blog comment]. Retrieved from http://studentbranding.com/the-Millennial-generation-do-you-fit-the-mold/

Twenge, J. M. (2010, February 18). A review of the empirical evidence on generational differences in work attitudes. Journal of Business Psychology, 25, 201-210. http://dx.doi.org/10.1007/s10869-010-9165-6

Volunteers in police service. (2015). Retrieved from http://www.theiacp.org/VIPS

Wasilewski, M. (2011). Taking on low morale. Retrieved from http://www.officer.com/article/10227600/taking-on-low-morale

Welsh, M. J., & Brazina, P. R. (2010, Fall). Gen y anatomy lesson: They're not alien, just different [Journal]. Pennsylvania CPA Journal. Retrieved from http://search.proquest.com.proxy1.ncu.edu

Welsh, P. (2005). DRT: Are police agencies dead right there? Law Enforcement Today. Retrieved from http://lawenforcementtoday.com/tag/police-culture

Wexler, C., Wycoff, M. A., & Fischer, C. (2007, June). Good to great policing: Application of business management principles in the public sector. Police Executive Research Forum. Retrieved from http://www.cops.usdoj.gov/Publications/good_to_great.pdf

White, M. D., & Escobar, G. (2008, March-July). Making good cops in the twenty-first century: Emerging issues for the effective recruitment, selection and training of police in the United States and abroad [Journal]. International Review of Law Computers & Technology, 22(1-2), 119-134. doi: 10.1080/13600860801925045

Wilson, James Q. (1985). Thinking about crime. New York, NY: Vantage Books.

World Future Society. (2007). Retrieved from http://www.wfs.org/ffn07stephens.htm

Yeaton, K. (2008, April). Recruiting and managing the 'why?' generation: Gen Y [Journal]. The CPS Journal, 68-72. Retrieved from http://search.proquest.com.proxy1.ncu.edu

About The Authors

Stephen M. Hennessy began his law enforcement career in 1962 as an administrative employee with the Federal Bureau of Investigation in Washington, D.C. After a year in Washington, he returned to home to Colorado working in the Denver FBI office. In 1966 he was appointed a Special Agent with the FBI servings in Houston, Texas, and Newark, New Jersey. Steve returned to Minnesota in 1973 and joined the Minnesota Department of Public Safety as Director of the Cooperative Area Narcotics Squad until 1977, when he was appointed an Assistant Superintendent in charge of investigations for the Criminal Apprehension Division. In 1984, he became responsible for the laboratory, information systems, finance, budget, and planning of the division until his retirement in 1991.

In 1993 he joined the Phoenix, Arizona Police Department, as the Training Advisor at the Phoenix Police Training Academy and worked designing various training programs, doing research, and handled special projects until he retired in 2003. He was the key instructor for the International Association of Chiefs of Police in the cultural awareness and racial sensitivity field from 1993 through 2003. He then joined St. Cloud State University, St. Cloud, Minnesota as a faculty member of the Department of Criminal Justice teaching in the undergraduate program and the Master's in Public Safety Executive Leadership program until he again retired in 2014.

Dr. Hennessy holds a bachelor of science in Business Administration from the University of Denver, a master's degree in Public Safety Education, Curriculum and Instruction, and a doctorate in Educational Leadership from the University of St. Thomas in St. Paul, Minnesota. He was the lead author of "A Cultural Awareness Trainer's Manual for Law Enforcement", a chapter author to "Multicultural Perspectives in Criminal Justice", and has authored numerous articles on cultural awareness training. He also authored "Thinking Cop – Feeling Cop, a Study in Police Personalities." He was a community faculty member of Arizona State University teaching in the School of Public Affairs, and with Northern Arizona University in the Master's in Educational Leadership program. He was a 2003 Martin Luther King "Living the Dream" award recipient from the City of Phoenix, AZ.

James R. DeLung started his law enforcement career at the Phoenix Police Department in 1994 after obtaining his Bachelor of Science Degree in Criminal Justice from Northern Arizona University in Flagstaff, Arizona. James received his master's degree in Educational Leadership from Northern Arizona University.

Dr. DeLung, while with the Phoenix Police Department, was assigned the tasks of teaching, writing, and delivering Cultural Awareness classes throughout the department and for the Arizona Peace Officer Standards and Training Board (AZPOST) statewide. After tours of duty in downtown Phoenix patrol, planning and research, crime statistics sergeant, and tactical operations center for terrorist activity sergeant, James transferred to AZPOST as the advanced training supervisor for all 167 agencies in Arizona.

While at AZPOST, James supervised and co-authored training for the 102-hour Arizona Leadership Program, culture awareness, generational leadership and communication, police response to persons with mental illness, creating and maintaining an ethical work environment, conflict management and source identification, effective team development, introduction and advanced police supervision, emotional intelligence, organizational socialization, culture, and change, self-determination and individual motivation, and

DiSC Personal Profile. James has a lifetime criminal justice teaching certificate for the Maricopa County Community Colleges. He also received an award from the City of Glendale, AZ as Honorary Chief of Police in 2009. James honorably retired from the Phoenix Police Department in April of 2014.

In May of 2015, Dr. DeLung completed his doctor of philosophy (Ph.D.) in Business Administration – Organizational Leadership from Northcentral University in San Diego, CA. He authored "Examination of Factors for Workplace Satisfaction of Millennial-aged Police Officers" as his seminal dissertation to complete his doctorate. His dissertation was published in the United States of America's Library of Congress. Currently, James is a Police Administrator on the Executive Staff of the Prescott, AZ Police Department as well as an international public speaker and trainer for both private and government organizations.

Made in the USA
Middletown, DE
22 February 2024

49625318R00119